Someone to Believe In

Someone to Believe In

G.G. Walker

Trilogy Christian Publishers A Wholly Owned Subsidiary of Trinity Broadcasting Network
2442 Michelle Drive Tustin, CA 92780

Rights Department, 2442 Michelle Drive, Tustin, CA 92780

Trilogy Christian Publishing/ TBN and colophon are trademarks of Trinity Broadcasting Network.

For information about special discounts for bulk purchases, please contact Trilogy Christian Publishing.

Trilogy Disclaimer: The views and content expressed in this book are those of the author and may not necessarily reflect the views and doctrine of Trilogy Christian Publishing or the Trinity Broadcasting Network.

Manufactured in the United States of America

10 9 8 7 6 5 4 3 2 1

Library of Congress Cataloging-in-Publication Data is available.

ISBN#: 978-1-64773-249-3

E-ISBN#: 978-1-64773-250-9

Dedication

This book is dedicated to my husband, Richard,

for inspiring me to put my stories on paper.

You encourage me to be obedient to God's calling

and to chase my dream of being a writer.

Your support means everything.

Thank you for believing in me.

Chapter One

Colorado Territory

Spring, 1870

"Chester! Stop that!" Nathan Lindquist shoved the dog away from the barn door. "I can't open it with you in the way!" He swung the big door open wide.

"Don't you go runnin' off, neither." Nathan wagged his finger in the dog's face. "I'm not gonna chase you again." Chester crouched and growled at the darkness inside the barn. "Do you hear me?" The dog inched his way inside.

Nathan crept forward. He wiped his brow with his elbow. Maybe it was a racoon. Or a mountain lion! Boy, howdy, this was his chance to show Ma that he was the man of the house. That old Willie Thompson would just about choke on a cherry pit if Nathan Lindquist captured a wild animal all by himself.

He grabbed the pitchfork from the pile of hay and caught up with Chester. Aw, it was probably nothing. After all, that old barn creaked and groaned a lot even if there wasn't a good wind. And at night it was plain spooky. Ma said there wasn't anything there in the dark that wasn't there in the light. That made sense—

until Nathan had to go in the barn after dark. Alone.

Something was sprawled out behind the pile of hay in the corner. Too big to be a mountain lion. Nathan inched forward until his toe kicked something. He froze. The lump on the floor moaned and stirred. Nathan scrunched up his face and peered at the floor. He'd kicked a rifle. And next to the rifle was a man.

Nathan ran like his shoes were on fire. "Chester, get out the way!" He dodged the mutt but stumbled and almost went down. He couldn't fall. Not now. The house never seemed so far away before. He made it! He jumped the width of the porch and twisted the kitchen door knob with both hands. "Ma! Ma!"

"Nathan! You know you don't burst into the house like that!" Carrie Lindquist dropped the spoon in her hand. "What happened? You look like you just saw the devil!"

"Ma." Nathan swallowed hard. "There's a man in the barn, and he's hurt real bad. You gotta come!"

"'Have to come.'" She eyed her son. "Nathan Lindquist, are you making up stories again?" If so, this was the best one yet.

"No, Ma. I promise!"

"Hmm." Carrie scanned the yard from the open door.

If there was a man in the barn, how'd he get there? What did he want? Was he dangerous? *If only Peter was here.* Sometimes she missed him so much. Carrie shook the menacing thoughts from her mind and lifted the rifle from behind the door.

"Nathan, you and your sisters stay in the house. Do you hear me?" She turned to look at her children. Six-year-old Abigail and three-year-old Emily stood like statues beside Nathan who was still shaking. Carrie squeezed the rifle to stop her own hands from shaking.

She stepped onto the porch and closed the door behind her. If ever there was a time for one of Nathan's wild stories, it was now.

Chester barked and raced toward her. "Quiet, Chester. That's enough out of you." She waved him away but he beat her to the barn door. "No, you stay out here." The dog whined and jumped sideways. She grasped the rough timber door, still standing ajar, and eased it open.

"Huh?" Something flew by her legs. One hand flew to her chest while she managed not to drop the rifle in the dust with the other. Just the cat. "Oh, Sadie! You scared the life out of me!" The hair on the back of her neck prickled. *Take a deep breath. Swallow.* She looked at Chester and pointed at the barn. "Well, come on. You're so anxious to go in there." And she wasn't anxious to go in by herself.

The dog leaped through the doorway, sniffing and growling his way through the dark. Carrie strained to spot anything out of the ordinary in the dark interior of the barn. Nothing was out of place.

A low moan slithered across the floor. She shuddered and raised Peter's rifle. "Who's there?" That horrible sound came from behind the straw pile. She pointed her weapon and crept forward.

"Quiet, Chester. Your whining is not helping." A few more steps. "What's that awful smell?" Carrie plugged her nose and peeked around the corner of the straw.

There on the floor. A man. A big man. Nathan was telling the truth this time. Chester sniffed the stranger and growled. Carrie knelt beside him, holding firm to the rifle. She shook the dirty, sweat-soaked shoulder of his shirt.

"Hey, mister. Mister, can you hear me?" She shook his muscular shoulder again, harder. "Mister!" Another moan.

She bit the inside of her lip. What was she supposed to do with him? He couldn't stay there in the dirt. A straw bed in one of the stalls? That was it. Then, if he died, at least he'd be out of sight of the children.

Carrie stood and started for the door, but stepped on Chester's paw. She jumped, and the dog yelped and bolted. "Oh, Chester! You're always underfoot. Stay out of the way!" She stepped into the sun, and there stood Nathan. Ten feet from the barn. "I thought I told you to stay in the house."

"Did you see him, Ma? Did you see the man?"

"Yes, I did. And he's hurt. I need to get some bandages." She hurried toward the house.

Nathan ran to catch up. "Can I help, Ma?"

"No. You stay in the house. And I mean it this time!" She threw a frown over her shoulder as she opened the kitchen door.

"Mama, is there really a man in the barn?" Abigail's eyes were as wide as silver dollars. "Does he have candy?"

"No, Abby! He don't have no candy." Nathan rolled his eyes.

"'Doesn't have any candy.' What would your father say if he heard you speaking that way, Nathan?" Carrie rummaged through the rag box for something to use for cloths and bandages. How many did she need, anyway? She gathered a wad of cloth in her apron. "This will have to do for now."

She lifted the water kettle from the stove and started back for the barn. "Remember, you stay here." She pointed her finger straight at Nathan. He nodded as she pulled the door shut behind her.

Back inside the barn, the light from the lantern did little to dispel the gloom that hung in the air. Carrie lifted the meager light over the wounded man. It was bad. What on earth happened to him? What kind of trouble was he in? Was it with the law? Her breath caught in her throat. Please, no! She couldn't go through that again. Ever.

She knelt in the dirt, took his whiskered chin between her fingers, and turned his head. A long scratch showed through the stubble, but it didn't look too bad. His arms and right leg felt solid. More scratches, but no broken bones. But his left pants leg and boot were soaked with blood. Maybe his leg was broken.

His wounds needed to be cleaned and bandaged properly, and that wasn't going to happen in the barn. But that meant moving him into the house. With the children and herself. What if he was dangerous? But if he had any chance at all...

She stood and looked down at him and smirked. "Well, at the moment you don't look very menacing." But what about when he got better? *If* he got better. Well, Peter wasn't there, but his rifle was. Loaded and ready.

Carrie hurried back to the yard. "Nathan!"

The boy peeked through the curtains before he opened the door. "Yeah, Ma?"

"Come on. I need your help. Get the potato cart and bring it into the barn."

"Really?" His eyes grew wider. "Yes ma'am." He darted off, following instructions.

"Hmm, he's never that excited to do his chores." She cocked one eyebrow and sighed.

"Here, Ma." Nathan came running pushing the cart toward her. "Is he hurt bad, Ma?"

"Yes, he is. You were telling the truth. This time," she finished under her breath. "Now come on." She led the way back into the barn.

She stood over the man, put her hands on her hips, and chewed the inside of her lip. How were they ever going to move him?

"Here, Ma." Nathan dropped the back of the cart in the dirt. "Wow, he's big!"

She reached for the handles of the cart and positioned it as close to the man's head as possible. "Now, listen. I'm going to wrap my arms around his chest, and when I tell you, I need you to lift his feet. Then I'm going to walk backward and we're going to lay him in the cart. I hope." She chewed her lip.

Nathan hurried to his appointed spot.

"All right. You ready?"

He nodded.

"Okay." Carrie bent and tried to slide her arms under his shoulders. He was even heavier than he looked. She groaned as she worked her arms under his, and around his chest. She paused and took a deep breath.

"I'm going to lace my fingers across his chest, and then we'll lift him. Okay?"

Nathan nodded again. "Okay, Ma." He waited, with his hands on the man's ankles.

"All right. On three. You ready?" Ready or not, they were going to lift him. She took another deep breath. "One… two… three!" She groaned and strained with everything she had. "Lift, Nathan. Lift!"

"I am! He's heavy!"

Where was that blasted cart? "Ooph!" Her foot got tangled in the wheel. She stumbled and almost dropped the injured man. Regaining her footing, she encouraged Nathan. "Almost there. Just a couple more steps." He couldn't give up on her now.

Then her thigh connected with the cart handle. "Ow!"

"Ma, are you okay?" Nathan's breathless voice just carried over their burden.

"Yes. Here." She laid the man in the cart. "We made it."

"He's too long. His legs are hangin' over." Nathan dropped the man's feet.

"I know. Can you hold them up while I pull the cart?"

"I guess so."

"Sure, you can. Here we go." Carrie's leg trembled as she turned the cart around and began to pull it toward the barn door and the house.

Finally, they were outside. Ah, sunshine. And fresh air. Carrie sat the cart down to wipe her hands on her apron. She wiped her brow with the back of her hand.

"Ma, I'm tired." Nathan wiped his own hands on his pants.

"I know. I am too. But the worst is over. We only have a little farther to go. We can do it. Come on." She lifted the cart handles and nodded encouragement.

"If you say so." He lifted the man's feet and followed along. "Chester, stay out of the way."

"Just a little bit more. There. We made it." To the porch, anyway. She all but dropped the cart handles.

"Don't just stand there." Nathan ordered Abigail and Emily. "Me and Ma got work to do. Get outta the way."

"Nathan, don't talk to your sisters like that. But girls, I need you to run and turn down my bed covers." They stared in disbelief. "Hurry!" The two girls scrambled to do as they were told. Carrie turned her attention back to the cart. "All right, we're going to lift the cart onto the porch. Ready?"

Nathan lifted his load again.

"One… two… three." They grunted and groaned, but somehow, they got the cart through the kitchen door.

Nathan dropped the man's feet. "I can't carry him anymore. He's too heavy, and I'm tired and thirsty."

Carrie sat the cart down and put her hand to the small of her back and stretched. "I know, Nate. Go ahead and get a drink of water." She could use a drink herself. But she needed more than water. "I can move him the rest of the way."

"Are you sure, Ma?"

"I think so." Maybe. Nathan had already done more than any eight-year-old should have had to do. She lifted the cart one more time and pulled. It didn't budge. She took a deep breath, yanked, and grunted. It moved, maybe an inch. She put her head down and pulled. The cart lurched forward, almost knocking her off her feet. "Whoa."

Nathan grinned at her from the other end, with the man's feet in his hands. "Just a little farther, Ma."

Tears sprang to her eyes and she nodded. Carried pulled and Nathan pushed, and they crossed the floor inch by inch.

At last, her bedroom. "Okay, put the cart by the side of the bed and we'll just roll him over. Here we go."

They put their hands on the man's side and with a big shove rolled him out of the cart and onto the bed. "Phew! We made it." Carrie shook her arms to get the blood flowing again. "Are you all right?" She eyed her son.

He seemed to have suffered no harm. Was that a gleam of pride in his eye? He had a right to be proud of himself. She was proud of him, too. He was growing up in spite of her. She smiled to herself and turned back to the man on the bed.

"Well, if he wasn't almost dead before he probably is now, after all of that jostling to get him in here."

"Ma, do you think he's a bad man?" Nathan's voice was almost a whisper.

"I'm sure I don't know, but don't let your imagination get the better of you." She began to unbutton the man's tattered shirt. "Go heat some water. When it's hot, bring me a pitcher full, and some of those clean bandages." The boy continued to stare at the man on the bed. "Nathan, go!" Carrie shook her head. That boy and his imagination. Maybe he wasn't so grown up after all.

"Look out!" Nathan scolded his sisters again as he pushed past them in the doorway.

The girls! Carrie looked into their ashen faces where they stood in the doorway clutching hands. She'd seen that fear in their eyes before. She'd vowed her babies would never see it again.

"Abigail, take your sister and go play in your room."

"Mama?"

"It's all right. Go ahead." She nodded and gave them a weak smile. Abigail led Emily away without a word.

The stranger's breathing was shallow and labored. At least he was alive. Carrie felt his forehead. Hot as a fire poker. "We'll have to get that fever down. I hope you like willow bark tea." The less severe wounds would have to wait.

What about his leg? How bad was it? She removed his bloody boots and his left sock, stiff with dried blood.

She retrieved her scissors from her sewing basket. Holding the hem of his pant leg firmly, she began cutting upward. The blood had made the tweed so stiff she could only snip a little at a time. Her hand ached from the effort by the time she reached his knee. So far, there was a lot of blood, but no wound.

She looked at the man's face and her own grew warm. "Thank goodness you're unconscious."

She began snipping the pants above his knee. Three more inches revealed a bullet wound. And it was infected. That explained the smell and the fever.

Carrie removed the rest of the pant leg. She took a deep breath and reached for his leg. She slid her hand beneath it and lifted it just enough to inspect the underside. A second hole. Good, the bullet went through. She released his leg and then her breath.

Nathan stood in the doorway with the pitcher and a cloth. He looked shocked. Was it the man's injuries, or the fact that he was now half undressed?

"Thank you, Nate. Bring the water over here and pour it into the bowl." She motioned to the table at the bedside. "Did you find some bandages?"

Nathan nodded and rounded the end of the bed. He poured the hot water into the big ceramic bowl on the table and set the pitcher and a clean cloth beside it. "I'll get the bandages."

He turned to go without looking at his mother or the bed.

"Get the honey too, please?" She picked up the cloth and dipped it in the water. "Yeow!" She yanked her hands back. Well, she had told Nathan to make it hot. She smiled and wrung the cloth with her now red hands.

Carrie began to wash the man's face. She tried to be as gentle as possible but he protested, even in his fever-induced stupor. Nathan returned with the bandages and honey and laid them on the bed without a word.

"Thank you. Now, why don't you take your sisters outside? The sunshine will do you good."

"Okay." The boy answered without looking up and left the room, closing the door behind him.

Carrie cleaned the wounds on her patient's face and arms, changing the water many times. The gash on his forearm needed more attention, but at least it wasn't infected yet. She tied off a bandage and wiped her brow. She held the small of her back as she straightened up.

Now for that leg. She had a fresh pitcher of hot water, clean cloths, and a bandage soaking in honey. Carrie took a deep breath. "All right, mister, here we go."

She took another breath and began cleaning his leg. What

was dried blood and what was dirt? It was hard to tell. The man on the bed began to growl and thrash like a wounded animal. His arms flailed above her head. She reached for his hands and missed. His arms came down, wrapped around her and pulled her with him as he fell back onto the bed.

"Ooph!" She landed on top of him, with her face next to his on the pillow. His arms relaxed, and she managed to untangle herself. She jumped up and looked down at the man, wiping her hands on her apron.

"Well, that's enough of that!" She re-pinned a loosened curl and caught her breath before she touched her warm cheeks with her hands. She put her hands on her hips and surveyed her patient.

"Thanks to your antics, you managed to open your wound. I guess that's a good thing. Now I can clean it better." Carrie knelt by the side of the bed again and began washing the blood and pus away from the hole in the man's leg. It smelled awful. How long had it festered, anyway? She turned her head and took a deep breath to keep from gagging. She didn't dare lose her breakfast. One mess was enough.

She stood up and stretched her aching back. She was wet and almost as bloody as her patient. "That's as good as I can do." Why was she even talking to him? Somehow it calmed her nerves. Nerves. Of course; that explained why her face was still so warm.

"I'm almost done." She pulled the bandage from the honey and wrapped it around the man's leg. Then she covered it with another bandage and tied it off.

She opened the window and filled her lungs with fresh air. So much better. She dropped into the tableside chair and wiped her face and hands with her apron. The lace curtain fluttered in the breeze and tickled her cheek. She brushed it away and studied the man in her bed.

At least he was calm again, and his breathing had slowed. But the flexing muscle in his jaw gave him away. She sighed and leaned back in the chair. He'd need a lot more care, but for now, he needed sleep.

She forced herself to her feet. "Well, I've done what I can." She rested her hands on the footrail of the bed. "You're in God's hands now… whatever good that'll do."

Chapter Two

Travis McCallister lay awake, eyes closed. His head pounded like a hammer on a wagon hoop. Every strike brought another throb. He forced his eyes open to a squint and began to survey his surroundings.

A small room; nothing fancy. He lifted his head and looked toward his feet. He blinked and tried to focus. A window with lace curtains. Maybe it *was* fancy. Then two cherubic faces met his gaze. Were they angels? He raised his hand to his eyes and lay back on the pillow.

Had he died? Was this heaven? Wasn't heaven supposed to be grander than one room with lace curtains at the window? And only two little angels? The Bible described it so differently. He tried to take a deep breath but set the hammer in his head off again.

"Girls, you shouldn't be in here." An attractive woman entered the room, whispering. "You'll wake…" She glanced at him and stopped mid-sentence. "Oh, hello. You're awake. I'm sorry if they disturbed you."

"No, I… uh… where am I?" he stammered, and tried

to swallow.

"Well, right now you're in my bed." A wry grin softened the sides of her mouth.

The fog in his head was so thick. None of this made any sense. "Mm. But where?"

"Just outside Cedar Creek."

"How long... have... have I... been here?"

"Well, Mr., um... I'm sorry, I don't even know your name."

Her voice was gentle, soothing. What *was* his name? "Um... Travis..."

"Well... Mr. Travis, I..."

"No. Travis... Muh... McCallister."

"Oh. Well, Mr. McCallister, I'm Carrie Lindquist. These are my daughters, Abigail and Emily." She introduced the cherubs, placing her hand on the head of blond curls, then the one with brown curls. "My son, Nathan, found you in our barn. You were hurt pretty badly. We had quite a time getting you in here. I was afraid we'd killed you for sure."

"How long have I been here?" he repeated, not much faster than the first time.

"The better part of three days. How are you feeling?"

"Mmm." He moaned and closed his eyes. How did he feel?

Like he'd been run over by a freight team.

"Do you think you could eat something? I have some soup on the stove."

He shook his head and winced. That was a mistake. The hammer banged louder.

"Well, would you like some water? You must be thirsty."

His mouth felt dryer than the Kansas prairie in August. He nodded, with his eyes still closed. He opened them again as she moved to the bedside table, poured a glass of water, and held it to his lips. "Here you are. Slowly. Not too much."

He looked into her eyes. They were like the eyes of a doe in the forest. Soft, kind, comforting. Then the room began to spin, and he closed his eyes to stop it. It didn't.

"You should rest now. I'll leave the door open a bit. Call out if you need anything. Come on, girls. You need to stay out of here."

Then the room was quiet.

Travis stared at the ceiling. How long had he slept? At least the insufferable anvil had stopped ringing in his head. And the fever was down, if not gone altogether. Now the searing pain in his leg demanded his attention. What happened? Oh, yeah.

It all came back. The rattlesnake. His horse spooked. His gun went off. The bullet pierced his leg. That's what happens when you don't pay attention. Let your mind wander. What a blame fool.

He pushed himself up against the headboard. How bad was his leg? It had been days. Gangrene could be setting in by now. He'd seen it too many times. Soldiers losing limbs, even dying. He forced the ghastly images from his mind.

Travis unwrapped the bandage and lifted the poultice. Honey? Interesting. He'd never used honey. He laid the bandage on the side table, took a deep breath, and let it out. The hole went clean through. That was good. It was infected. No wonder it was so painful. The infection was clearing, though. Whoever had cleaned and bandaged the wound knew what they were doing. Barring the unexpected, it should heal fine. He leaned his head back and sighed.

Thank You, Lord, for preserving my life, and for bringing me here to these people, and for the help they have given me. And…

The chatter of children interrupted his prayer. Three children, right? A boy and two girls. And what was their mother's name? He searched his foggy memory. Carrie Lindquist. That was it. *Thank You, Lord, for Carrie Lindquist and her children.*

"Ma, can I play with the kittens? Please?"

"We'll see, Abigail. Eat your lunch first." Carrie set a glass of milk in front of her oldest daughter.

"You're too little, Abby. You don't know how to handle 'em. You might hurt one of 'em," Nathan pointed out.

"I wanna see 'em too, Mama." Emily nibbled her sandwich.

"'Want to see them.' Emily, you're beginning to sound just like your brother."

"Can we see 'em, please?" Abigail wouldn't give up.

"We'll see. You need to finish all of your lunch first."

"But, Ma, they don't know…"

"Nathan, that's enough. Your sisters will be very gentle. Besides, the kittens are big enough now that they'll be fine."

Carrie's bedroom door creaked open and Travis McCallister emerged, struggling with the buttons on his shirt. "Do you mind if I join you?"

"Mr. McCallister, what are you doing up? If you're hungry, I'd be glad to bring you something." Carrie jumped up to help him.

He leaned on her shoulder and staggered to kitchen table.

"If I stay in that bed much longer, I think I'll lose my mind. I'm not used to being laid up." He pressed both hands on the table for support.

"Nathan, get another chair," Carrie ordered, as she reached for a plate and silverware.

"Thank you very much, young man." He groaned as he lowered himself into the chair. "Oh… that feels better already."

"Children, stop staring. It's not polite." Carrie laid the place setting on the table. "Well, I guess you haven't been properly introduced. I don't know if you remember, but my name is Carrie Lindquist, and this is Abigail and Emily." She motioned to her daughters. "And this is Nathan. He's the one who found you in the barn." She pointed to her son. "This is Mr. McCallister." She added nodding toward their guest. "Can you say hello?" She reminded them of their manners.

"Hello," they answered in unison.

"Hello. I'm glad to meet all of you. I remember meeting a pretty lady and two little angels, but I thought I had died and gone to heaven." He winked at the girls and of course, they giggled. He tried to draw a deep breath but winced at the effort. "And I'm glad to meet the man who saved my life by finding me." He smiled at Nathan.

Nathan's face turned red as he dropped back into his chair. "Ma didn't believe me when I told her."

"Well, I don't blame her. It's not every day someone just appears in your barn."

Carrie sipped her coffee, eyeing the man over the rim of her cup. He seemed nice. Maybe he was just trying to earn her trust. Or was he trying to win over the children first?

Travis cleared his throat. "I understand that you all have some kittens. How old are they?"

"Six weeks." Nathan wiggled in his chair.

"Sis weeks." Emily wanted to be heard, too.

"Do you wanna see 'em?" Nathan filled his mouth with sandwich.

"'Do you want to see them?'" Carrie shook her head. Where had he learned to speak that way?

"I would. But maybe another day. The walk to the table was enough for now."

His smile was easy. Maybe too easy.

"Are you an outlaw?" Nathan was blunt, as usual.

"Nathan. That's rude! I'm so sorry, Mr. McCallister." What he must think of Nathan's manners? But was he an outlaw? She wanted to know the answer to that question, too.

"No, I'm not." He looked around the table. "But that's a fair question. It must look pretty bad, the way I appeared out of nowhere."

"If you say you are not wanted by the law, I believe you. You don't need to explain." Carrie tried to sound convincing. She wanted to believe him.

He continued, ignoring her comment. "I was riding across the prairie, east of here, when a rattlesnake spooked my horse. He went crazy and ended up bucking me off. I fell off and dropped my rifle. It went off, and the bullet hit me in the leg. And that's the truth. I feel like a greenhorn, getting shot that way."

"So how did you find your way here?" Carrie wanted all the details now.

"I don't know. I remember climbing back into the saddle. I must have blacked out after that, because the next thing I remember was waking up in your feather bed." The tips of his ears turned red and he cleared his throat.

Maybe he wasn't a criminal. Did criminals blush? She didn't think so.

He looked across the table at his hostess. "I want to thank you for all that you have done for me. I suppose I'd be dead otherwise."

"You're welcome, Mr. McCallister. I'm just glad we were able to help."

"Travis."

"I beg your pardon?"

"Please, call me Travis."

"Oh. All right."

"I just wish I knew what happened to my horse. He was the best one I ever owned. We've been together a long time. Seen a lot of places."

"Well, there was a roan out in the field right after you arrived. I assumed he was yours, judging from the amount of blood on his side and on the saddle."

"Really? That's him! Oh, thank the Lord." Relief washed over his face.

"Nathan and I took care of him and put him in a stall in the barn."

"Thank you again. It seems I'm more and more beholden to you and your family."

"May I be 'scused?" Abigail interrupted.

"Have you finished eating?" The little girl nodded. "Finish your milk, and you may go. And, you may go see the kittens after you clear your dishes."

All three children drained their glasses and jumped from their chairs. They hurried to put their dirty dishes in the sink and headed for the door, which even in their haste they remembered to close.

"They're good kids, Mrs. Lindquist." Travis smiled at the closed kitchen door.

"Thank you." She was proud of them. "And, you may call me Carrie."

He smiled and nodded. "Thank you for the loan of the clothes." He tugged on the sleeve of his shirt. "It's a little snug, but I appreciate your husband sharing with me. Will he be home soon?"

She gripped her coffee cup. "Why do you ask?"

"I'd like to thank him for his hospitality. It must be hard for him to have a strange man in his home and sleeping in his bed." A boyish grin turned up the corners of his mouth.

Carrie looked down at her hands as her cheeks grew warm. "My husband…" She raised her eyes to meet Travis'. "Peter is dead. He was killed in an accident two years ago."

Chapter Three

"Oh. I'm sorry. I didn't mean to... um... I..." Travis tried to undo his social blunder. How could he take back his words? "It must be difficult raising three children alone."

Carrie stood and began clearing the table. "I manage." She gave a slight shrug of her shoulders. "You should probably lie back down. You don't want to overdo on your first day out of bed."

"I think I'll just sit here for a while, if you don't mind. I really don't like being laid up." He looked around the large single room. The front door opened into the kitchen, but to the left of the door was a sitting area, complete with fireplace and two rocking chairs. Three rooms opened off of the opposite side of the kitchen. The first was the bedroom with the lace curtains. Were the other two bedrooms as well? Most likely.

"You have some well-crafted pieces of furniture." He nodded toward a hutch against the wall by the bedroom door. "That hutch, this table and chairs, the sideboard... Someone is a real craftsman."

Carrie looked up from the dish water. "Yes, my husband

Peter built them. He was a woodworker."

"I can see that. Did he hand carve the dresser in the bedroom, too?" Was she always this aloof? Or was it just him? Of course, who could blame her? She didn't know anything about him or where he came from.

"Yes, he did." A smile crossed her face. She looked up again with pride in her eyes this time. "He made that for me when we got married. He was a fine craftsman."

"I don't doubt it." Travis emptied his cup.

"Would you like more coffee?" Carrie reached for the coffee pot simmering on the stove.

"No, thank you." He held his hand over his cup. "I've had enough for now. By the way, the doctor did a fine job of fixing up my leg. I'll have to thank him, too."

"Doctor? We don't have a doctor. Not since Dr. Sprague retired and moved back east, anyway."

"Then who cleaned and dressed my wound?"

"I did."

"You? How did you know… where did you learn how to take care of a wound like that?"

"My father's father was a doctor, and I followed him everywhere when I was a girl. I remember some of what I learned from him about treating wounds. And I've had a little practice, living out here. One of my three is always finding a way to get hurt."

"Well, thank you. I thanked the Lord for sending me somewhere that I could get help, but to send me to someone with medical training... I'll have to thank Him again." He smiled, trying to show his gratitude.

Carrie turned back to the sink of dirty dishes and her back stiffened.

"Well, I think I've done enough for today. I better go back to bed."

"Do you need some help?"

"I think I can make it." Travis pushed himself up from his chair. Even his good leg wobbled. Was it going to hold his weight? Maybe he really had overdone it. Maybe he did need help. He shook his head.

"Thank you, anyway." He had to do this on his own. He had to push himself if he was going to get better. But it was a long way back to the bedroom.

Questions. All she had were questions, and few answers. He said he wasn't wanted by the law. That was a relief. But where did he come from? Was he from around here? If not, what was he doing in this part of the country? Did he have a family? Someone must be wondering what had happened to him.

She was frantic the night Peter disappeared. She had feared he was lying somewhere, hurt, and no one knew to tell her. Then came the awful truth. She shuddered. Another woman wouldn't go through that, if she could help it.

She knocked on the bedroom door. Hearing a soft "Come in," she opened it and entered the room. "Mr. McCa... um... Travis, I hate to bother you, but could I talk to you for a minute?"

"Sure." He used his arms for support as he sat down on the bed. "What's on your mind?"

Did he always have to be pleasant? For some reason it irritated her, but she brushed it aside. "I was just wondering if there's anyone I should tell that you're here. I mean, your family must be worried about you. I could send a telegram to let them know that you're alive and well."

"No, there isn't. There isn't anyone to worry about me."

"Oh." No one? There was no one who would be worried? "Well, I just wanted to know."

"Thank you, though." He eased back on the bed.

"Well, I'll let you rest." She left the room and closed the door behind her.

There was not a soul on this earth who cared whether he lived or died? How sad. How lonely he must be. She knew lonely.

Chapter Four

Travis watched the children from the rocking chair on the porch. He loved children. They were so honest and full of life. If he and Elizabeth had been able to have children… That old ache flared in his soul, and he shook his head. No sense in looking back. He couldn't risk disturbing those demons that would again threaten to devour him. No, it was best to let them sleep.

"It's my turn." Abigail clutched the cloth ball.

"No, it's not, Abby. You had your turn. It's Emmy's turn." Nathan tried to wrestle the ball away from her.

"You always skip my turn." Abigail's lower lip protruded, and tears welled up in her eyes.

"Don't cry, Abby. It's still Emmy's turn."

A tear slid down her cheek. "Oh, take your dumb old turn, Emily." She threw the ball hard toward her younger sister. "But then it's *my* turn!" She pointed to herself with her thumb.

Travis clasped his hands and twisted his thumbs. If all disputes could be settled like those of children, they wouldn't have had to fight that horrible war. The nation wouldn't have been torn apart. Elizabeth would still be alive. He sucked in a breath and shook his head again. Those beasts began to stir. He couldn't allow them to torment him anymore.

He turned his attention to the Lindquist farm, or what was once a farm. The barn door gripped its hinges, waiting for the next storm to hurl it across the prairie, and the whole thing needed a new coat of paint. The fence that was still standing wouldn't keep out a stiff wind. And an abundant crop of weeds choked out any chance for something useful to thrive in the field. Then there was the house. It was solid, but neglected as well.

The children's laughter filtered in through the window. Carrie rubbed one of Abigail's dresses on the washboard. How did those three manage to get so dirty? Their laundry added so much to the washing from her customers; sometimes it seemed the laundry would never be done. Or any of the chores. It was more than one person could do, and it seemed her best just wasn't good enough. At times, it was all she could do to make it through another day and then collapse into bed. Carrie sighed and put her wet hands to her back as she straightened. She rubbed the cramped muscles, but it didn't help.

How good to hear the children laughing and playing. They hadn't laughed much since their father had been gone. Were they well? Were they happy? Their cheery voices encouraged her mother's heart. Carrie lifted the basket of wet laundry and headed for the door.

"Hey, can I help you with that?" Travis pushed himself out of his chair as she exited the house. "That must be heavy."

"Oh, no. I can manage." Somehow it didn't seem as heavy today.

"Ah, come on. At least let me help you a little. After all, I need to earn my keep." He took the basket from her, stepped off the porch, and limped his way toward the clothesline.

His gait was much better. It wouldn't be long before he'd be moving on. That was fine. She'd gotten pretty good at making do. She really didn't need help from anybody, for anything.

"Do you need me to hand you the clothes?" Travis set the basket down.

"No thanks. I don't want you to overdo." She hung the first garment on the line. "Abigail and Emily usually help me. If I let you do their chores, they might get the wrong idea."

"Well, just this once, then." He smiled and winked and picked up the next piece of wet laundry.

She cleared her throat, took it, and swung it in place. One by one each piece of clothing was hung to dry in the breeze, as if the souls of their owners inhabited them.

"There." Travis handed her the last shirt in the basket.

Carrie hung it on the line and swiped the wrinkles out of it. "Thank goodness. I don't know which is worse, wash day or ironing day," she sighed.

The clatter of wagon wheels got their attention, and they watched a buggy turn off the road and enter the yard. Carrie gasped, and her breath caught in her throat.

"Who is that?" Travis whispered, as the buggy stopped in front of the house.

"Samuel Washburn," Carrie choked out.

"Who's he?"

"The banker." She almost spit out the answer. Why was he there? Never mind. She knew. She knew this day would come, but not today. Not today. She willed her feet to move as she trekked to where the banker set his high-top shoes in the dirt of the farm yard. "Children, go inside." She spoke without looking at them. "Now."

Travis escorted the children into the house and closed the

door. Whatever was happening between Carrie and Samuel Washburn was not his business. But the three bewildered faces staring up at him were.

"Why don't we set the table for lunch?" He rubbed his hands together, trying to lighten the mood. "Nathan, you do the plates, Abigail and Emily, you can do the cups, and I'll do the forks and spoons."

But he stole a peek through the curtain anyway. There was no need to hear the conversation. Fear and worry etched Carrie's face. Her outstretched arms pleaded for something. But what?

"Do you have the spoons, Travis?"

"Huh?"

Nathan stood in front of him with his hands out, just like his mother in the yard. "Do you have the spoons? I'll put 'em on the table if you want."

"Oh, yes, I have them. Here you go." Travis handed the utensils to the boy and followed him back to the table.

Carrie's stomach churned hot and her head vibrated with each heartbeat. Samuel Washburn never drove out to see her, or anyone, with good news. "Hello, Mr. Washburn. Can I help you?"

She wanted to scream at him to go away. To leave them alone.

"Hello, Mrs. Lindquist." His icy voice almost cracked. His beady eyes bulged from their sockets and his mustache twitched. He looked like a weasel as he wiped his lip with his handkerchief. He shoved it back in his pants pocket and squinted at her. "Yes, you can help me. As you know, the bank has granted you an extension on the mortgage on your farm, dependent upon you making proper payment."

Straight to the point. Quick and painless. For him, anyway. "Yes, and I am very grateful."

He withdrew a document from his vest pocket and unfolded it. "However, the last payment is now ten days late, and according to your agreement, your loan has now become due and payable as of the end of the month."

Carrie stared down at her clenched hands for a brief moment. She inhaled and straightened herself. "I know the payment is late. I have half of it, and I can give it to you now. I'll have the rest by the end of the month." Somehow, she had to get the money by then.

"That will not do. The payment must be made in full." He wiped his lip again. "At the end of the month, you will have ten days to vacate the property."

Her heart plummeted to her shoes as she forced herself to focus through the buzzing in her head—the buzzing from a swarm of angry bees. "But Mr. Washburn, I have three small children. Where will we go? They've lost so much already, you can't take away their home!" Her eyes stung with tears. She bit the inside of her lip and tasted blood.

"I'm sorry; my hands are tied," he replied without emotion, then turned and climbed into his buggy. He clucked to his horse. "Good day, Mrs. Lindquist." He drove past her and back onto the road without so much as a sideways glance in her direction.

Carrie didn't hear his farewell over her heart pounding in her ears. A whirlwind of thoughts swirled in her mind. What were they going to do? Where could they go? What would she say to the children? *Peter, why did you leave us?* She trudged back into the house like a horse that knows its way back to the barn.

Carrie leaned against the door, pushing it shut with her weight, her expressionless face the color of some of the undergarments she'd just hung to dry. She swayed her way to the table and grabbed the back of a chair.

Travis stood still, unsure of what to do. Should he make his presence known, or try to leave the room without notice?

"Mama, we set the table for lunch." Abigail stood tall with her little chest out and a broad smile on her face. Nathan shot her a look that would wither sunflowers, but that didn't matter. "Mama, can we...."

"Don't you have chores to do?" Carrie spat the words in their direction.

"Well... we... yes." Nathan's voice was low and timid.

"Then go do them!" Carrie's knuckles were white on back of the chair. Nathan and Abigail started toward the door.

"But, Mama... I don't have any chores." Emily's little voice broke, and tears filled her eyes.

"Then help your brother."

Emily hung her head as she followed her siblings. Carrie reached out as she passed and cupped the little girl's chin in her hand. She lifted Emily's head and half-smiled at her. The children left and closed the door behind them. Carrie sank into the same chair she'd clung to and dropped her head into her hands.

Good. Travis' opportunity to disappear. The kitchen door was too far away—he'd have to pass by Carrie to get to it.

The bedroom was closer. A few steps and he'd be out of sight. He tip-toed into the bedroom and closed the door without a sound.

He let out a heavy sigh as he sat on the edge of the bed. Just what had the banker said to Carrie? Whatever it was had upset her. No. It had unnerved her. Well, whatever the problem, it was none of his business. There was nothing he could do. As soon as he was able, he would be leaving. But he could pray.

Lord, please help Carrie and her children. I don't know what the trouble is, but You do. You own the cattle on a thousand hills. All creation is Yours. Whatever the problem, I know You have all the power to solve it. Father, if I can be of use to You in this place before I leave, here I am. Thank You, Lord. Amen.

Chapter Five

At last, the children were in bed. Why did they seem to fight the hardest when she needed them to go to sleep the most? Carrie filled her cup from her mother's silver teapot, the one treasure she had left from her childhood. Her mother's stories paraded through her memory. Stories of how her great-great-grandfather had bought the silver tea set in Boston for his wife before the turn of the century. And how it had been handed from mother to daughter, travelling from Boston to Missouri, and then to Colorado.

Her mother had divided the set between Carrie and her sister, Grace. Carrie had the teapot, but Grace had the cups. The two of them had shared many afternoons over tea, until Grace's family moved to Red Dale.

Carrie stirred in two spoons of sugar and carried the brew outside to the porch. She settled into her favorite rocking chair. The one Peter made for her.

It was a beautiful night; the kind of night that renews a weary soul. Carrie took a deep breath of the cool air, drinking it in. She pulled her shawl a little tighter to keep out the late spring chill and took a sip of her tea.

"Mind if I join you?"

Startled, Carrie looked up to see Travis standing in the door. "No, no, please do." He crossed in front of her and took the rocking chair next to hers. Peter's chair. Carrie cleared her throat before she spoke. "How's your leg?"

"It's mending."

"That's good. Do you have any pain?"

"No, not really. It aches a little when I'm on it too much. But that'll pass."

They rocked side by side for a few minutes, the silence broken by the creak of the porch under their weight.

"It sure is a beautiful night." Travis studied the sky. "The stars look like flickering candles."

"Yes, it is. I love to sit here and watch the stars and listen to the crickets." Her voice trailed off as she drifted away into her peaceful refuge.

"This is a nice rocker. It's well made. Very comfortable. Did your husband make these?" He rubbed the arms of his chair.

"Yes, he did." She caressed the arms of her own chair.

"He really did beautiful work."

"His work was known throughout the county. He made a

good living for us." She was still proud of him.

"I'm sure he did." He paused for a breath. "I want to thank you again for everything you've done for me."

"You're welcome. I'm glad that you're doing better and that your leg is going to be all right."

"Me, too. But I feel really guilty about moving you out of your room for so long."

"Oh, don't worry about that. The girls love it when I sleep with them, anyway." They were getting spoiled. It was going to be hard to move back to her own bed.

"I would like to repay you somehow. I don't have much money. But I do have time. A lot of time. So, I would like to do some work around here. Whatever you need done."

"Really? I… I… thought you would be leaving as soon as you were able to ride. I mean, don't you need to be getting home?" He wanted to stay? Why?

"I don't have a home. Not anymore, anyway. I'm a travelling man of sorts. I ride from place to place and stop when the Lord tells me to stop."

"The Lord tells you to stop? How do you know? I mean, does He actually speak to you?"

"In a way. Sometimes I feel like Abraham—you know, in

the Old Testament. I go until I reach the place that God has for me, although I don't pretend to be nearly as righteous as Abraham."

Carrie swallowed a laugh and forced herself not to smile. "Oh, I don't believe you. How does God talk to you? Like we're talking now?"

"No. I just hear His voice in my spirit."

From what she knew of God, she didn't want to hear anything He had to say, even if she could hear Him. Her mother's instinct shouted to send Travis McCallister on his way. He had seemed steady as a rock until now. But he was a loon!

"I'm not insane, I assure you."

Was he a mind reader, too?

"I travel where the Lord leads me and sojourn there as long as He can use me. Then I move on. He has faithfully supplied all of my needs, and I have received more blessings and joy than I could have imagined."

"What did you do before you...?" How should she put it? "Before you began this... journey? Where did you come from?"

"I hail from Pennsylvania. I had a business near Pittsburgh."

"What kind of business?"

"Just a small one. I shuttered it during the war." A shadow crossed his face.

"Were you in the war?"

Travis nodded. The war had left its mark on so many. "Soldier's heart," they called it. That could explain his hearing voices. "Did you fight for the North or the South?" It seemed important, for some reason.

"I served in the Union Army." He looked down at his boots.

"So, how long have you been travelling around the countryside?" She really was interested now.

"Since the war ended. Five years now." He let out a heavy sigh. "I've been many places and seen many things. I've met some very interesting people. And I have seen God work in ways that I would have never believed possible." He spread his hands wide.

"So, you believe that God told you to stay here?" He had to be mistaken. "I can assure you that God is not at all concerned with my needs or my children's. If He was, He would not have taken Peter away from us." Her anger threatened to erupt.

He rubbed his palms in time to the crickets. "I'm so sorry, Carrie. No, God hasn't told me to help you. But I would like to repay you for your kindness and hospitality by doing a few repairs. And it won't cost you anything, except supplies and a few meals. I'll more than pull my weight. I'll even do my own laundry." He tugged on his shirt front and chuckled.

Well, he seemed sincere, even if he was a loon. And he was right. She needed help, more than he knew. She cleared her throat and looked at him. "There's a room off the barn that was Peter's workshop. I could clean it up and put a bed in there for you. It should be warm enough this time of year."

"That would be just fine. Do we have an agreement, then?"

"Yes." She shook his outstretched hand and half-returned his smile. "Well, I should get to bed. I'll start working on that room in the morning." She stood and turned toward the door. "Good night."

"Good night, Carrie."

She changed in the darkness of the girls' bedroom and crawled into Abigail's bed. What had she done? He didn't fool her with that "wish to repay your kindness" ploy. The entire farm was in danger of collapse. Anyone with eyes could see that. She couldn't keep up with the work, and there was no money to hire help. So maybe it was a good thing that Travis McCallister landed in the barn.

Chapter Six

Carrie eased the door to Peter's workshop open and surveyed the room. Stepping inside, visions of Peter flooded her memory. The pungent smell of fresh cut wood and the sweet aroma of beeswax filled her nostrils. Peter's blond hair hung in his face as he ran the plane over a piece of wood. He looked up and smiled and his blue eyes twinkled, his face covered with sawdust. She gasped. If she reached out, she could touch him.

"Where would you like me to put these tools?"

"What?" Peter? No, Travis. Peter was gone, and her heart ached all over again.

"These tools. Where do you want me to put them?" Travis lifted the tools from the hooks on the wall.

"I'll take care of those." They were Peter's. They were sacred.

"Oh, okay. Well, then, I'll go work on repairing my bed." He jerked his thumb toward the barnyard.

"Fine." He left, and she picked up the broom.

The spiders had made themselves at home. Carrie almost hated to ruin some of the spiders' artwork. Cobwebs and dust shrouded the entire room. A shroud like the one she had used to bury her heart. You shouldn't disturb the dead.

Carrie knocked on the door before opening it. A shaft of lamplight spread out into the darkness of the barn, with little impact. She stepped into the small room, the door still open behind her.

"How do you like it?" Travis spread his arms to display the results of their efforts.

More images of Peter flashed through her memory. He smiled at her and took the cup of coffee she brought him as he worked late into the night. His tools hung on the hooks on the wall. No, wait. They were gone. Clothes hung there now. Travis' clothes.

"Carrie? Are you all right?"

"Hm? Oh. Oh, yes, of course. You finished the bed!" She forced herself to focus and to ignore the gnawing in the pit of her stomach.

"Yeah, it needed a lot of repair, but it's comfortable and sturdy now." He smiled with pride. "Are those for me?" He nodded toward the pile of bedding in Carrie's arms.

"Oh, yes." She remembered the reason for her visit. "I brought you some extra blankets in case you need them." She handed the pile off to Travis.

"Thank you. I can't imagine needing them right now, but I might later."

"Will you be all right out here?"

"As happy as a bear in a cave." He grinned, rubbing his hands together.

She smiled. An awkward silence settled between them like a blanket. Carrie cleared her throat. "Well, I better get back in the house and finish putting the children to bed. If you need anything else, just let me know."

"Thank you. I will."

"Well, good night."

"Good night, Carrie."

She breathed in the night air as she strolled back to the house. It was nice to have a man around again. Too bad he wasn't staying long.

Chapter Seven

Carrie pulled the wagon to a stop in front of the general store and set the brake. She'd avoided the bank. Now if she could do the same with Mr. Washburn, it would be a good day.

Travis jumped down and reached up to take her hand. Carrie hesitated, but took his outstretched hand and climbed down from the driver's seat.

"Cedar Creek is bigger than I thought." Travis set Emily on the boardwalk and reached for Abigail.

"Well, it is growing, but most folks don't live in town. We have a mercantile, a feed store, a telegraph, a blacksmith, a church, and of course, a saloon." Carrie smirked and began loading bundles into her arms.

"What about the bank?"

Carrie hesitated. "And the bank." She didn't even look in his direction. "Nathan, keep an eye on your sisters while I deliver this laundry." She loaded the last of her packages.

Nathan jumped from the back of the wagon to the street. "Aw, Ma, do I have to?"

"Yes, you have to." Her heart ached. It wasn't fair for him to have to shoulder so much. He was only eight. But what would she do without him?

"Do you need some help carrying those?" Travis eyed her load.

"No, I'll be fine. Thank you." Did he think she was helpless?

"Well, then, I think we might find something to do while we wait." Travis removed his hat and ran his hand through his hair.

"Really?" Nathan's eyes lit up.

"Really." Travis grinned and winked at Carrie.

Carrie frowned at him. "I don't want to have to bail my children out of jail."

He raised his right hand in solemn oath. "You can trust me." He couldn't contain his smile.

"I dearly hope so. I should be done in about an hour. I'll meet you back here at the wagon?"

"Sounds like a plan." Travis nodded. "Shall we go?" He herded the children like they were little chicks.

Carrie watched the children scamper along the boardwalk ahead of Travis. "You can trust me," he had said. No one in Cedar Creek could be trusted with her children. So, why should she believe Travis McCallister? And why did she?

"Well, hello, Nathan, Abigail, Emily. How are all of you today?" The rotund, balding man behind the counter held his arms out in welcome.

"Hi, Mr. Dawson." Nathan shoved his hands in his pockets. "Fine, thank you." He led the way to the counter where the three of them lined up, intent on the man behind the numerous jars of candy. So many tasty treats.

The three of them looked like soldiers from the war, countless ones still children themselves. Excited. Innocent. Unaware of what was to come. So many of them gone. Too many young lives cut short.

"What's your pleasure today?" Mr. Dawson's voice broke through Travis' thoughts.

"I'm not sure their mother wants them to have any candy." Travis stepped forward.

"Oh, all the youngsters can expect a treat when they visit Dawson's store. My wife always scolds me. She says we're losing money and spoiling the children." His belly shook as he chuckled. He spoke in a voice only Travis could hear. "But I think they all need a little spoiling, especially these three." His voice boomed again. "All right. What'll it be? Mr. Nathan wants a licorice stick, and Miss Abigail, you like lemon drops." Their heads bobbed as they reached for their preferred confections. "Now, Miss Emily, will it be a peppermint stick or gum drops?"

"Gum dops." Emily stood on her toes to see over the counter.

"Very good. There you are." He had no more than handed her the treats before she popped one in her mouth. Mr. Dawson chuckled and then sighed. "Too bad you can't hand out joy like candy."

"Thank you, Mr. Dawson." Nathan remembered his manners. His sisters' mouths were too full to speak.

"Oh, you're welcome." The jolly man turned his dancing eyes on Travis. "I don't believe we've met. I'm Jack Dawson. My wife, Martha, and I own the store."

Travis shook the man's outstretched hand. "Travis McCallister."

"Are you new in these parts?"

"Yes, I am."

"Are you a friend of Mrs. Lindquist's?" He paused. "I'm sorry if I seem overprotective. It can be dangerous for a widow alone with three young ones, living so far from town."

"I'll save you the trouble of fishing for information. I

was injured on the trail and somehow found my way to the Lindquist's barn. Mrs. Lindquist tended my wounds and has allowed me to stay in her home while recovering." He finished with a level look. Was that a good enough explanation? Well, that's all he was going to get.

"She must have done a good job. It seems you're well enough. Are you planning on staying around for a while?"

"A while. I'm going to do some work around her farm to repay my debt, so to speak, before I move on."

"That's very decent of you. She could sure use the help. Well, welcome to Cedar Creek."

"Thanks." Jack Dawson's curiosity seemed satisfied—for now, anyway. Carrie had enough trouble. She didn't need the neighbors spreading gossip about the stranger in her barn.

"Speaking of work, I need some supplies for the repairs." Travis pulled a list from his shirt pocket and handed it to Dawson. "And do you know where I could buy some laying hens?"

"Laying hens? What do you want with laying hens?"

"I have an idea I want to explore."

Chapter Eight

"Hello, Mrs. Marsh." Carrie smiled at the frail, white-haired woman who opened the door. "I have your laundry."

"Hello, Carrie. What was that?" The woman squinted and leaned on her cane as she peered up at Carrie.

"I have your laundry," Carrie repeated louder. "Do you want me to put it away for you?"

"No, Maude's here. She can help me do it."

"Oh, okay." Carrie entered the little home and put the bundle on the table across from where Mrs. Marsh's neighbor, Maude Trendle, sat. "Hello, Mrs. Trendle. How are you?"

"Hello, Mrs. Lindquist. I'm well." The woman eyed her through wire-rimmed glasses as Nettie Marsh left the room. Maude Trendle always looked like she had just sucked a lemon, and her pointy nose made her look like a bird. "I've heard that you have an unexpected visitor out at your place."

Was that a question, or a statement? How was Carrie supposed to answer that? Did she even want to?

"Here you go, Carrie." Nettie Marsh returned, with her clutched hand held out in front of her. She deposited two dollars into Carrie's open palm.

"Oh, Mrs. Marsh, this is too much. You never have that much washing." Carrie shook her head and pressed the money back into the frail little hand.

"No. No, it isn't. You are such a help to me."

"W... well, thank you very much! That is so generous."

"Nonsense. Use it to buy those sweet children of yours something special."

Carrie dropped the coins into her purse and smiled at the old woman. She was a dear. "Well, I better be going. I have more stops to make." Carrie reached for the doorknob and opened the door. "Thank you again, Mrs. Marsh."

"Bring those children with you next time. I'd love to see them." Nettie Marsh waved.

"It was nice to see you, Mrs. Trendle."

The old crone nodded and grinned. "You, too, *Mrs.* Lindquist," she muttered, with an emphasis on the Missus.

Carrie pulled the door shut behind her and stepped off the porch. Thank goodness Mrs. Marsh's perfect timing had ended Mrs. Trendle's hunting expedition. The old bird dog was on the scent of a tasty tidbit. She should have tucked a napkin in her collar.

"Carrie!"

Carrie looked up to see Liza Martin hurrying toward her. A smile erased the frown on her face. "Liza, how are you?" She obliged the petite woman with a halfhearted hug.

"I haven't seen you in weeks. Are you making deliveries?" Liza squeezed Carrie's arms.

"I just finished with the last one."

"You look tired." Liza studied her friend's face. "What's wrong?"

Carrie shrugged and shook her head. "Oh, Maude Trendle was at Nettie Marsh's when I delivered her wash."

"And?"

"She asked about the visitor at my house. Thank goodness Mrs. Marsh interrupted her before I had to answer her question. How does she even know there's a visitor at my place?"

"Carrie, everybody in town has heard about the man at the Lindquist farm, thanks to your nosy neighbor."

Carrie rolled her eyes and groaned. "Esther Shafer. I saw the Shafers and their brood going by on the road last week, but I didn't think anything about it. I should have known."

"Who is he, anyway?"

"Liza! You, too?"

"Well, I'd like to hear truth instead of just rumors."

Carrie crossed her arms and pursed her lips. "All right. His name is Travis McCallister. Nathan found him injured in the barn about two weeks ago. He was so bad I didn't know if he'd even make it. But he pulled through. And now he's helping me with some repairs to pay me back."

"How long is he staying?" Liza asked. Carrie huffed and glared at her now. "I'm just asking." Liza held up both hands in defense.

"He'll leave as soon as the repairs are finished. They should be done in about two more weeks."

Liza studied Carrie. "Are you sure it's such a good idea? Him staying at your house and all?"

"He's not staying in the house. We made a room for him in Peter's old workshop."

"But wouldn't it be better if he stayed in town?"

How many more questions? How many more rumors? "Liza, Travis is working on my farm, like any other hand. Would any other farmer have their hand stay in town?"

"No, I suppose not. I just…"

"Just what?"

"You know I'm just worried about you. I guess all I can do

is try to stop the rumors when… I mean, *if* I hear any."

"I hope I can count on that." Carrie squinted and raised one eyebrow.

Liza crossed her heart and held up her right hand in oath. "I will do my best to correct any wrong information I encounter."

"I have to go. Travis and the children are waiting on me. Thank you for being my ally. I'm counting on you." Carrie gave her friend a proper hug and hurried away.

"Ma!" Nathan jumped up from the boardwalk and ran toward his mother.

"Hello." Carrie hugged him close with one arm. "Have you been good for Travis?"

"Yes, ma'am." He grinned up at Travis.

Carrie eyed the man she had left in charge of her children. "Well?"

"Well, what?" Travis turned his attention from Nathan to Carrie.

"Well, did they behave?"

"Of course, they did. Why wouldn't they?"

"Hmm, somehow I think leaving you in charge is like leaving Nate in charge of the candy jar." Carrie gave him a sideways look as she lifted Emily into the wagon.

Travis' smile reached his eyes. "Sometimes, you might be right. But not this time." He helped Abigail get settled in the wagon.

His laugh. So rich and full. The back of Carrie's neck tingled, and her stomach fluttered like butterfly wings. She gathered her skirt and scampered into the wagon seat before he could help her up. She grabbed the reins and held them loose in her hand.

"Everybody in?" Travis asked the children as he climbed up and reached for the reins. "Good. Here we go."

She thought for a moment and then handed him the reins. Why not? If he could be trusted with her children, he could handle a team. He hesitated then took them, clicked his tongue, and the horses moved out.

"I met Jack Dawson today. He seems like a good man." Travis looked over at Carrie. She stared straight ahead.

"Yes. He and Mrs. Dawson are nice people. They spoil my children, but they're nice."

He had to approach this the right way. If he could convince Carrie to try his idea, and if it worked, it would be good for her family.

"I asked him where a person could get some laying hens. I've been thinking. If you buy three or four good hens, after a few weeks you could sell the extra eggs."

He stole a glance at Carrie. She was staring at him, expressionless. Did she hear him? Did she understand his plan? "Well, what do you think?"

"Chickens? Really? Chickens have to eat, you know. How am I going to feed them? And what makes you think I want to be in the egg selling business? And where would I even sell these eggs?" Her voice rose in volume with each question.

Travis swallowed. One thing for sure, Carrie was long on resistance. "Chicken feed is cheap, and they can also eat scraps from the garbage pail. As for selling them, Jack Dawson already said he'd buy them for the store." He adjusted his hat. "It won't make you rich, but it will bring in a little money. Enough to make a difference, anyway."

"How do you propose buying these hens? Every penny I have is already spent."

"Let me figure that out. Are you willing to try it?" He studied her face. "If it turns out to be a bad venture, you can have fried chicken for supper." He grinned and chuckled.

She wasn't amused. Her stare almost bored a hole in him, but she didn't say no.

Chapter Nine

Travis looped the reins around the rail in front of the church and patted his horse's flank. He was early, but the anticipation of attending a church service again was too much. He retrieved his Bible out of his saddlebag and rubbed his hand over the worn cover.

"Well, hello. I'm Esther Shafer." A large woman introduced herself. "This is my husband, Lemuel." The man shook Travis' hand without a word. "This is our oldest, Leah. And this is Josiah and little Martha, and over there are Caleb and Amos." She pointed in the direction of two young boys scampering through the growing crowd.

"Travis McCallister. I'm pleased to meet all of you," he replied, with his hat in his hand.

"You must be new to these parts." Lemuel Shafer squinted his eyes under the brim of his hat.

"Yes, I am."

"Aren't you the man we've seen at the Lindquist farm?" Esther Shafer's smile was almost accusing.

"Seen?"

"Esther, don't pry." Lemuel was hushed by a withering glance from his wife.

"Are you a friend of the Lindquist's?" The woman's eyes narrowed a bit.

"You could say that." Esther Shafer was a persistent woman. Nosy, even. "Are you a friend of Carrie's?" Travis studied her from under the brim of his hat.

"Oh, my, yes. We've been neighbors for years. That's how we've seen you. We were going by on our way into town."

The bell in the steeple announced the start of the service.

Lemuel took Esther's arm. "We better get inside. Come on, children. Time for church." He steered his wife toward the front stairs while herding his little flock toward the church doors.

Travis inhaled and blew it out. *Thank you, Lord, for the bell ringing when it did. Your timing was perfect, as always.*

"We'll have to have you and the Lindquists to dinner soon," Esther continued over her shoulder.

Travis didn't respond as he mounted the church steps. Inside, he surveyed the room. White pews lined both sides of the aisle, which led to the altar. Stained glass windows lit the room with a rainbow of colors. Beautiful.

The Shafers filled a pew close to the front. But Travis took a seat in the back, near one of the colorful windows. Maybe there he could go unnoticed.

A young lady in front of him turned and smiled, as did her mother. Another young woman eyed him from across the aisle. So much for going unnoticed. Travis pulled at his collar. Where was the preacher?

"Good morning, everyone. I'm glad to see all of you here today." A middle-aged man stood and raised his arms in welcome. "Let us stand and sing 'Beautiful Savior.'"

Good, a hymn Travis knew well. He sang along, with his full baritone drawing even more admiring looks. The heat from his face crept down his neck, under his already too-tight collar. The girl across the aisle didn't sing a note for watching Travis. She needed to practice her spying skills.

"Thank you, everyone. You are all in fine voice this morning. Please be seated." The preacher waited for the commotion to cease before he continued. "Psalm 139:23-24 (KJV) reads, 'Search me, O God, and know my heart: try me, and know my thoughts.'"

Ah, one of Travis' favorites. He mouthed the words as the pastor finished reading, "And see if there be any wicked way in me, and lead me in the way everlasting." Was there any wicked way in him?

Father, if there be any wickedness in my heart, I confess that to You. Please forgive me. I only want to do what is right in Your eyes. Lord, whisper in my ear. Speak in my heart. Travis continued praying, eyes closed.

Movement around him brought his prayer to an end. He looked up. Everyone was on their feet. The sermon was over? He had missed the rest of it. The sweet melody of "Amazing Grace" filled the room. Another good hymn. Travis rose to his feet and joined in, loud and strong.

The preacher greeted each person with a smile and a handshake as they passed him at the door. "Hello, I'm Reverend Chandler." He reached his hand out to Travis.

"Hello. Travis McCallister."

"I'm glad you could join us today. Are you new to Cedar Creek?"

"Yes."

"Have you just settled here?"

"Not really. I'm helping a family for a little while, then I'll be moving on."

"Anyone I might know?"

"Maybe. The Lindquists."

"Oh, yes, Carrie and her children. Well, I'm glad you are there to assist her. I have offered my help many times, but she has always refused. I think she's really struggling on her own."

"Yes, she is. Well, thank you, Reverend Chandler. It was a pleasure to meet you."

"Same to you, Mr. McCallister. And if there is anything I can do for the Lindquists, please let me know. I really would like to help."

"Thank you. I'll keep that in mind." Travis swept his hat onto his head and descended the stairs. *Lord, if there is anything Reverend Chandler can do for Carrie, please show me, and bring her to be accepting of it. Amen.* He climbed into the saddle and walked his horse toward the edge of town.

Carrie called from the porch as Travis rode into the yard. "Hello. You're just in time. Lunch is ready." She wiped her hands on her apron.

"I'll be right in." He rode into the barn, dismounted, and put his horse into a stall. "I'll be back after lunch, fella, to unsaddle you. I don't want to keep them waiting." He patted his steed on the rump and left the barn.

"Hi, Travis." Nathan greeted him with a smile as he entered

the kitchen.

"Well, hello."

"Where'd ya go?"

"Nathan, don't be rude. Travis is free to come and go as he pleases. He doesn't have to tell us his business." Carrie set fresh-baked bread on the table before taking her chair.

"I went to church this morning, Nathan."

"You did?"

"Mm-hmm. I met some really nice people. I even met your neighbors, the Shafers." He looked across the table at Carrie.

Her face was expressionless. "That's nice."

"They said they'd like to have all of us over for dinner soon." He waited for a reaction. There was none.

"Could we, Ma? I could play with Caleb and Amos." Nathan's eyes lit up like a firecracker.

"And Martha." Abigail squirmed in her chair and shoved a bite into her mouth.

"We'll see. There's no reason to get excited. We haven't been invited yet."

"I also met Reverend Chandler. He's concerned about all of you." Carrie put her fork down and leveled a look at him. "He said he'd like to help, but you've always refused his offer."

Carrie scowled and took a sip from her cup.

He would let it go for now, but not for long. "Well, thank you for lunch. If you'll excuse me, I better go take care of my horse." Travis laid his napkin on the table and pushed his chair back. He could use the fresh air.

Chapter Ten

Travis set the brake on the wagon and climbed down from the seat. The door of the farmhouse opened and a thin, stoop-shouldered, older man plopped his hat on his head and stepped off the porch. He had a noticeable limp.

"Hello. Are you Charlie Taylor?"

"I am. Can I help you?" The man's white beard bobbed as he spoke.

Travis extended his hand. "I hope so. My name's Travis McCallister. Jack Dawson said you might have some laying hens for sale."

"He did, eh?" The man wiped his long mustache with his finger. "I might consider it, for the right price."

The right price? Travis had no money. Neither did Carrie. God was going to have to provide. Well, the Lord had provided everything he had needed so far.

"Come in the house and we can talk." Charlie Taylor turned back to the house, and Travis followed him. Charlie held the door open for Travis and closed it behind him. "Edith! We have company."

"Be right there." Edith's voice drifted in from another room.

"Sit down." Charlie Taylor limped to a padded chair and lowered himself with care.

"Well, what do you know? It ain't often we get company around here." A short, rotund woman appeared, her cheeks red like ripe apples.

"This is the wife, Edith." Charlie Taylor removed his hat and hung it on the arm of the chair. "Edith, this is... What'd you say your name was?"

"Travis McCallister." Travis removed his hat and nodded. "Pleasure to meet you, ma'am."

"Would you like a piece of apple cake? I just took it out of the oven. I've been baking all morning." She wiped her brow with the back of a plump hand.

"That must be what smells so good. But no, thank you. I came to try to make a business deal with Mr. Taylor."

"He wants to buy some of our laying hens." Charlie Taylor eyed Travis.

"Wonderful! Well, Charlie, you were just sayin' that we need to have us some fried chicken 'cause we're getting too many hens." Edith's excitement didn't spread to her husband.

"Yeah, yeah. All right, young man. How many hens are you looking to buy?"

"I was thinking three or four, if you can spare them. The problem is, I have no money."

"No money!" The old man waved to shoo Travis away. "Then I'll thank you to not waste my time."

"Well, I'd like to suggest a trade."

"Trade? I doubt you got anything worth trading for." Charlie shook his head and rubbed his beard.

"I have time, and I'm willing to work. I'd be at your farm two days a week for as long as you say, and I'll do whatever chores you need done." *Please, Lord, move Charlie Taylor's heart to accept my offer.* "I noticed a woodpile out there that needs split and stacked. I could do that for you, and anything else you needed."

The man stared at Travis without a word for what seemed like eternity. "How did you know?"

"Know what?"

"I broke my leg last fall, and it ain't healed right. Still gives me fits." Charlie rubbed his right thigh.

"We been praying for God to send us some help." Edith Taylor spoke in a hushed tone. "You must be the answer to our prayers." Tears sprang to her eyes.

"Well, you would also be the answer to my prayers. I'm trying to help Carrie Lindquist. The hens are for her, to set her up in the egg business. It won't make her rich, but she could use any extra money right now." *Thank you, Lord.*

Chapter Eleven

Carrie exited the barn with a basket of candled eggs and stopped short. She was captivated.

Travis set the post and shoveled dirt around it to hold it in place. He leaned the shovel against the corral and wiped his brow with his bandana. He removed his hat and did the same with his head and hatband. He replaced his hat on his head and reached for a dipper of water from the bucket. A slight breeze stirred his shirt, hanging on the fence.

She gasped at the sight of a shirtless Travis. As he worked, she could see his muscles rippling under the late morning sun. She could see that he was no stranger to hard work. He was taller and stockier than Peter had been. He had dark hair, where Peter's hair was blond. Yet, his eyes were clear blue, like Peter's. She was transfixed. He looked around, and she was caught.

He reached for his shirt. "I'm sorry. The sun bearing down on my back feels like a blacksmith's forge." His face tinged red. "Are those eggs going to Dawson's?" He buttoned a few buttons.

"Yes. Yes, they're ready. I can take them in tomorrow when I take the laundry." She paused a moment. "You know that I really do appreciate your help in fixing this place up. I mean, you've barely recovered, and you're working so hard."

Travis grinned and chuckled. "You worried about me?"

"That you're doing too much? Yes. You've already re-hung the barn doors, fixed the gate and now the corral, not to the mention the chickens. And, I just don't know if it's worth it."

"Of course, it's worth it," he took another drink of water from the bucket hanging on the fence. "Why wouldn't it be?"

"Because the bank is going to take it away."

"Take what away?"

"The farm." She whispered the words.

"What? Why?" He dropped the dipper back in the bucket.

"I'm behind on the payments, and Mr. Washburn said that the board has decided that if I don't pay what I owe by the first of the month, they'll call in the loan. They'll foreclose." Carrie bit the inside of her lip to keep it from trembling. She hadn't told anyone about her conversation with the banker. Why was she telling Travis now? "I just don't want you to go to all of this trouble for nothing." She couldn't keep her voice from quivering.

They stared side by side over the fence out at the prairie. Travis broke the silence. "I had no idea the situation was so dire. I figured there was a problem, but foreclosure!" Silence again. "There has to be something we can do."

"It's going to take more than selling a few eggs, I'm afraid."

"I can only imagine how hard it's been since your husband died. What happened to him, anyway, if you don't mind me asking?"

She froze. No one had asked that question before. No one had dared. Could she trust him with the truth? Could she even talk about it? He'd proved trustworthy so far. She gripped a fence rail for support and took a deep breath. "Peter wasn't killed in an accident." She stared at the prairie again.

"I don't understand."

"About three years ago, Peter struck up a friendship with a drifter who turned out to be a wanted man. A bank robber. Somehow, he convinced Peter that he could get rich if he helped rob the bank in Parkdale. It's a town north of here. Peter never shared his plans with me. I have no idea what he was thinking. We didn't really have any money problems. We weren't rich, but we got by." She paused for another deep breath.

"So, one night they robbed the bank." She looked out over the fence. "Well, the posse caught up to them in one of the canyons up river. There was a gunfight and Peter was killed, along with one of the deputies." She ground her toe into the dirt as she bit her lip to fight back tears.

She checked for little ears that might be listening. "I just couldn't believe Peter would do such a thing. I still can't." Tears pooled in her eyes.

"You much have been devastated. You and the children."

"The children don't know. That he robbed a bank, I mean." She looked up at him. Tears spilled down her cheeks. "I told them that their father was killed in an accident. They were too young to know any different."

"But..."

"I couldn't have them growing up with the burden of knowing what their father had done. The shame of it. It's better that they don't know how he died." She squared her shoulders.

"I don't know what to say. I... am... so sorry. But that's a mighty big burden to keep all to yourself. What if the children should find out?"

"They won't."

"How do you know? I mean, people talk. You can't protect them forever."

"Then I'll do it as long as possible. Everyone close to them has been sworn to secrecy. And now that includes you." She glared at him.

"Your secret is safe with me," he vowed, raising his right hand in oath. "I would never breathe a word. I swear."

Carrie nodded and turned to walk away. She still wasn't sure why she told him. But talking to him was easy, almost comforting. She felt better for telling him her secret. Now she had to believe he was a man of his word.

Travis stared after her. The enormity of her secret weighed on his heart. What a burden. The death of Peter. Now she was losing her home. *What else, Lord? What more can happen to Carrie and her children?*

His heart ached for her. But was it just because of her sorrows? He wasn't blind, after all. She was a very attractive woman. He remembered looking into her warm brown eyes during his delirium—the same doe-like eyes that had just been filled with tears. Chestnut brown bangs framed her face like feathers. How long was her hair when it wasn't pinned up in a braid? But he had made a vow that he would not get involved. He'd be moving on soon. The thing to do now was pray. God had a plan to help Carrie and her children.

Chapter Twelve

Carrie breathed on her mother's silver teapot and wiped off the last smudge. There. Almost like new. Almost. She wrapped it in cloths and laid it in the bottom of the crate she used for her deliveries. And just in time, before Travis opened the kitchen door. He closed it behind him and went to the stove for a cup of coffee. She placed the laundry bundles on top and smoothed her hair.

"Are you all right?" Travis carried his cup to the table and pulled out a chair.

"Of course. Why wouldn't I be?" She wiped her hands on her apron and set the box on the floor.

"You seem a little jumpy." He sat down and took a sip from his cup.

"You're imagining things." Carrie waved off his concern and sat in the chair opposite him.

"I've been thinking about Mr. Washburn and the bank."

"What about them?" Her heart constricted in her chest.

"How much more time do you have on the loan?"

"Five days." Her mouth went dry. Five short days.

"I have an idea."

"Another idea? You want me to raise cattle now? No!" She held her hands up in resistance.

"No, nothing like that. I've been thinking about the field you have out there." He leaned back in his chair. "If we cleared it, we could plant crops that you could sell come harvest."

"Nothing grows in that field now but thistles. It would take a lot of work to reclaim it."

"But it can be done."

"And what am I supposed to raise? And how am I supposed to harvest it after you're gone?" She gasped. That last part slipped out. She hadn't meant to voice to her worry.

"You don't have to do everything alone, Carrie. You have neighbors who are willing to help."

Hmph! Neighbors. Nosy neighbors, like Esther Shafer? No, thank you.

"Besides, the crops wouldn't all ripen at the same time, so that would help. I was thinking of planting wheat and corn for sale. Then you could plant whatever vegetables you want."

"Crops take time. The loan is due now. Harvest is months from now."

"Do you have enough for the payment that's due?"

"I… will have." She pictured the teapot tucked in the box at her feet.

"All right. Go to the bank and give Washburn the money you have. Then, you promise him the proceeds from all sales of the wheat and corn."

She just stared at him. Maybe her first impression was right. Maybe Travis McCallister really was a loon.

"Do you want me to go with you?"

"What? No. I'll do it. But I think you're crazy—and don't be surprised if Samuel Washburn thinks so, too." Carrie nodded at him and rose from her chair.

Carrie's hand shook as she turned the doorknob and opened the door of the bank. There he was. Mr. Washburn, behind the teller cage, with his little mustache that seemed to twitch with the pleasure of handling money.

Two people were in line ahead of her. She had to wait. Her stomach knotted and unknotted a thousand times until it was her turn. She stepped up to the counter.

"Well, hello, Mrs. Lindquist. This is a surprise." The banker looked shocked.

Carrie controlled her urge to reach through the bars and

slap the insincere grin off his face. "Hello, Mr. Washburn. I've brought the payment that is due." She reached into her purse and removed the money she had, plus what she had just received from Mr. Dawson.

"That's all well and good, Mrs. Lindquist. But as I told you, the entire loan is due at the end of the month. One payment will hardly be enough."

"Yes, I remember." How could she forget? "However, I have an idea to present to you that will allow me to bring the loan current and stay in my home."

"Hmm, and how do you propose to do that?" The man looked at her through the wire-rimmed glasses that sat on the end of his nose.

Oooh! Little weasel. He was so smug in his self-made empire. Her ears felt like they were on fire. "I now own laying hens, and I have begun selling eggs in Dawson's General Store. And Mr. Muh… I mean, I am going to plant two crops, wheat and corn. Which I will harvest in the fall. I am willing to sign over all future proceeds from the sale of them at harvest."

He waved his hands to stop her. "Mrs. Lindquist, raising crops takes time, and selling eggs is hardly a lucrative venture." He folded his bony hands on the counter. "Your loan is seriously delinquent. The bank has been more than patient. The next step is foreclosure, and for you and your children to vacate the property."

Carrie slammed her hand flat on the counter, making the little man jump. "No! That is not the next step, Mr. Washburn." She swallowed hard to keep her voice from quivering. "Yes, you can choose to foreclose. And then you will have an abandoned farm on your hands, for who knows how long. I mean, people aren't exactly flooding into Cedar Creek just looking to settle down here." Good. She had his attention. "Or, you can choose to give me a chance to save my home. I'm willing to try. Are you?" She looked him square in the eye, daring him to reject her offer.

The only sound was the ticking of the big clock behind the teller cage. Samuel Washburn pursed his lips and wiped his mustache. "Very well. I have serious doubts, but I will defer the foreclosure for sixty days. If, in that time, the loan is brought current and kept current, you and your children may stay until the harvest is sold. However," he pointed a scrawny finger toward the ceiling, "if not, the foreclosure will take place, and you will be ordered to vacate. Is that understood?" The banker's eyes were dark slits in his wrinkled face.

"Yes. And thank you." Carrie turned to leave. She had to get out of that bank and away from Samuel Washburn. And she had to tell Travis. They had a long road ahead, but it was a start.

Chapter Thirteen

"How's it coming?" Carrie asked Travis, as she handed Nathan a dipper of water from the bucket. Nathan emptied the dipper and handed it to Travis, who plunged it back into the bucket.

"Good." Travis lifted the dipper to his lips and drained it, wiping his mouth with his sleeve. "We should be ready for planting by the first of the week." He wiped his neck with his bandana.

"It sure is a lot of work, huh, Travis?" Nathan wiped his own brow with the back of his hand.

"It sure is." He grinned and tousled the boy's hair. "Well, we better get back to work."

"Do we have to? I'm tired," Nathan moaned, and sank to his knees.

"You should be tired. You've done a man-sized job today. There isn't much left to do. I'll finish up."

"Travis, are you sure?" Carrie eyed them both. Was Nathan just trying to get out of work? The sweat streaks through the dirt on his face proved he'd earned a rest, and a bath.

"I'm sure." He shoved his bandana back in his pocket.

"Supper will be ready in about an hour."

"Perfect." Travis nodded and walked back toward the field.

Carrie hung the dipper on the bucket and wiped her hands on her apron. She helped Nathan off the ground. "You need to get washed up, young man, and I need to start supper."

"The corn is coming up already." Carrie pointed at the inch-high sprouts smiling in the sun.

"Sure. And over there is the wheat. And you can just see the potatoes, and carrots, and squash." Travis nodded in their direction.

"And the irrigation ditch you put in. Where did you learn how to do that?"

"A man in Kansas showed me how to do that. It'll sure save a lot of trips hauling buckets of water."

"I won't miss that." Carrie's arms and back still ached at the memory of carrying full buckets from the well to water the crops. "But it's so big. It's going to take a lot of work to keep up with."

"Nothing worth doing comes easy." Travis picked up the hoe and headed toward the vegetables.

"Mama, do we have to pull weeds?" Abigail whined from where she sat in the dirt.

"Don't whine, Abby. You know I don't like whining."

"But it's hot, and my feet hurt."

"Mine, too," Nathan put in. "And my back."

"I know it's a lot of work, but we have to keep the weeds from taking the field back over." Carrie put her hand to her own back and tried to stretch out the kinks. "Listen, if you finish two more rows each, I'll take you to the swimming hole."

"Really?" they asked in unison.

"Come on, Abby. Let's hurry and finish," Nathan called, as he ran off with his sister on his heels. They worked hard, refreshed by just the thought of going swimming.

"No, Abby, you don't pull the weeds that way. You do it like this." Nathan proceeded to instruct his sister.

"I wanna do it my way," Abigail insisted.

"But you can't. It's all wrong."

"No, it's not!" She stuck her lower lip out.

"What seems to be the trouble here?" Travis knelt beside them.

"Abby's pulling the weeds all wrong. She's just pulling off the tops. That's not the way to do it."

"Well, now. Let's see." Travis inspected Abigail's handiwork. "Mm-hmm. I see the problem."

"You do?" The little girl stood amazed.

"Why, these weeds are so stubborn that they don't want to give up their roots. But you have to show them who's boss and pull them out, roots and all." Travis demonstrated. "And I know you can do it, too." She nodded with enthusiasm. "Here, let's pull a few together so you can show me how."

Nathan shook his head and went back to work. "Girls," he muttered with disgust.

"Mama, here's a big weed." Emily grinned and held up a handful of potatoes just beginning to take root.

"Oh, Emmy! Those aren't weeds, honey. Those are potatoes. They won't grow if you pull them out of the ground." Her little face fell. "Oh, don't cry, sweetheart. It will be all right. Nate, will you help Emmy put these back in the ground?"

"Emily, you can't pull…" Nathan began, until his mother's cluck and scowl stopped him. "Come on. Show me where you found these so we can put them back." He used a softer tone with his youngest sister, though still tinged with disgust. Emily led him to where she had lifted the potatoes from the soil.

Carrie threw up her hands in mock surrender as Travis

approached. "She was only trying to help," he chuckled, and smiled.

"I know." Carrie sighed and tucked a wayward strand of hair back in place. "It's just… some days I don't need so much help." She grinned and sighed again. Travis hurried on with his task. "What's your hurry?" she called after him.

"I heard something about going to the swimming hole. I have to finish my two rows." He laughed out loud.

Carrie giggled to herself. He was a wonder.

Chapter Fourteen

Travis pulled the wagon to a stop in front of the blacksmith's. "I'm going to see about that axle."

"All right. Should I meet you back here when I finish my errands?" Carrie climbed down from the wagon seat.

"Sure."

"All right. Children, wait for Travis in the wagon."

Nathan scuffed the toe of his boot on a rough plank of the wagon bed. "Why do we gotta stay here?"

"'Have to stay here.' Honestly, Nathan, your grammar gets worse by the day. Because I won't be very long, and I don't want to have to round you all up when I get back."

"Ma, will you bring us a treat?"

"Abigail, you don't need a treat every time we come to town. I'll be back soon." Carrie sighed. They were getting spoiled. Nothing worse than a spoiled child.

"Well, hello, Carrie." A willowy blond met her on the boardwalk. "How are you today?"

"Oh, hello, Virginia. Fine, and you?"

Virginia looked past Carrie and eyed Travis. "Oh, fine and

dandy."

"How's George?"

"Hm? Oh, he's better. He was down sick last week, but he's on the mend now." Virginia glanced at Carrie, but then her eyes were back on her target, Travis.

"Travis?" Carrie called him over. "Travis, this is Virginia Hobart. Virginia, Travis McCallister."

Travis tipped his hat. "Pleased to meet you, ma'am."

Always the gentlemen. Carrie chuckled to herself.

"I've heard a lot about you. I mean, we heard that Carrie had a houseguest."

"Travis has been working for me." Virginia was fishing for information, and Carrie was not going to take the bait.

"Actually, Mrs. Lindquist was very kind to me and did me a great favor… So, I'm just trying to repay her kindness."

Mrs. Lindquist. Even Travis could see through this woman like glass.

"Oh, isn't that nice." She smiled like a cat about to pounce.

"Well, if you ladies will excuse me, I need to talk to the blacksmith." And with another tip of his hat, Travis was gone.

Virginia watched him until he was out of sight. "Carrie. Are you sure it's wise to have a man staying in your home?"

"I don't know what you mean." Oh, here it came. Steady, Carrie.

"Well, there's been talk."

"What kind of talk?" Just what was the latest tidbit? Virginia would be up on every detail.

"Well, it's just not proper, you being a widow and all... I mean, a lonely widow and an attractive man... alone... Well, you can see how it looks."

Heat flowed to Carrie's cheeks. Her ears burned again just like at the bank, and she bit the inside of her lip. "No, Virginia, how does it look?"

"You know... indecent," she finished in a whisper.

Carrie took a deep breath, and her hands curled into fists at her sides. "To set the record straight, Virginia, Travis has been working on my farm in return for room and board. And, furthermore, he is not staying in my home. He's staying in the barn. He has been a great help to my family, and that is all. Now, if you'll excuse me, I have things to do."

Virginia looked stunned, no doubt surprised that Carrie wasn't embarrassed and ashamed.

There had been talk, indeed. Gossip spread like prairie fire, and Virginia Hobart had fanned her share of the flames.

"Well, hello there." Jack Dawson looked up as the bell rang over the general merchandise door.

Travis entered, followed by Nathan, Abigail, and Emily. "Hello, Mr. Dawson." Travis smiled and closed the door.

"Please, call me Jack. No formalities around here." He turned to the children. "Well, now, what'll it be today? The usual?"

The children nodded their heads in unison. "All right, then." He handed each one their favorite treat and wiped his hands on his apron. "There you go. Enjoy them, kids."

"Thank you, Mr. Dawson." Nathan always remembered his manners.

"Thank you." Abigail remembered, after her brother.

"Tank you." Emily was learning.

"You're welcome." His big smile almost hid the big man's eyes.

"Are you spoiling the children again?" A woman with graying hair entered the store from a side door.

"Yes, I am."

"Well, hello, Nathan, Abigail, Emily." The woman smiled

at the children. "It's good to see you."

"Hello," Nathan answered, and the girls nodded.

"Oh, Martha, this is the man I told you about." Jack turned his attention to Travis. "Travis McCallister, this is my wife, Martha. I told her about how you're working to help out at the Lindquist's."

"It's a pleasure to meet you, Mrs. Dawson. Carrie has told me about you folks." He tipped his hat and smiled. Carrie actually liked the Dawsons, so they must be good people.

"I'm so glad to meet you. And I'm so thankful that you're helping Carrie. She needs the help, but she's proud and stubborn and has a hard time accepting it from anyone." Martha covered her mouth with her hand. "I shouldn't have said that in front of the children, but it's true," she added in a hushed tone.

She spoke the truth. Plain and simple. Except Carrie wasn't just proud and stubborn. She was scared and angry. All good reasons, in her mind, to keep people away. "Well, I'm doing what I can," Travis admitted.

"Can we go outside?" Nathan asked Travis, still sucking on his licorice stick.

"Okay. But stay right out front." Travis watched them close the door behind them. "By the way, Jack, do you have any sarsaparilla?"

"No, I'm afraid not. You have to get that at the saloon."

"All right." Travis glanced up to the shelf behind the counter, and something caught his eye. A silver teapot. It looked just like Carrie's.

"Something else I can help you with?"

"Huh? Uh… that teapot up there. It looks just like the one Carrie showed me. She said it was her mother's. How odd that there would be another one just like it." Travis shrugged and shook his head.

"There isn't. She brought that in here a few weeks back and asked if I'd like to buy it. I don't buy used goods as a rule. But it being silver…"

"But why would she sell it?"

"She said she needed the money." Jack dusted the counter.

The loan payment. Carrie had half of it, and said she would get the rest. That was her plan. Would nothing ever go right for Carrie?

Chapter Fifteen

"Hoowee, it's hot!" Travis wiped the sweat from his face with his sleeve. "We'll finish that garden fence today, though." He worked the handle on the water pump.

"Sure is." Nathan lifted his sweat-stained face and watched the water gush into the bucket.

Travis brought a dipper of water to his lips. After taking a drink, he flicked the rest of it in Nathan's face. Nathan sputtered and gasped for air.

Travis laughed out loud. "Feel better?"

Nathan giggled with glee and flung water from the bucket at his attacker with both hands. Travis refilled the dipper and poured it over the boy's head.

"WHAA!" Nathan sputtered and grabbed the bucket and swung it in the man's direction. He yelped again when most of the water missed his target and splashed in his own face.

"Aaaah!" Travis gasped. That water was cold. He gasped for air and tried to wipe the water from his eyes. "Good shot. All right, Nate. Now we're even." He laughed and shook the water from his hair.

"It wasn't me!" Nathan protested, standing in a puddle of his own making.

"Huh?" Travis looked up, water dripping from his nose. "Carrie!"

There she stood, kitchen bucket in hand, beaming from ear to ear.

"Why, you…" He pumped the handle with urgency. "Okay, if you want to play…"

"No!" Carrie laughed and began to run.

"Get back here." He grabbed her arm. She wasn't getting away that easy. He pulled her to him. There. He was soaked and now she would be too. He held her tight while Nathan splashed more water on her.

She squealed with delight and slipped her arms around Travis' neck. It was hard to say what was better, to hear Carrie's laughter or to feel her in his arms. She pulled away, but her warmth stayed with him. His breath came a little faster.

"I wanna play!" Abigail's lip couldn't stick out any farther.

"Me, too." Emily wouldn't be left out.

"Of course. Here you go." Travis splashed them a little and they giggled with delight. "There you go." He smiled and laughed. Such pure joy.

"Well, now that everyone's soaked to the skin, how about some cider?" Carrie dabbed her face with her apron.

"Yeah!" The children shouted and clapped.

"That sounds good," Travis agreed. "Hey, while your ma gets the cider, why don't we get dried off?" Nathan nodded his head and smiled as Travis ruffled Nathan's blond hair.

"Here you go." Travis handed the boy a towel from the nail in the barn. "It shouldn't take long to dry, as hot as it is."

"Boy, that was fun!" Nathan dried his face and hair. "Can we do it again sometime?"

"Sure." Travis shrugged on a dry shirt and began to button it. "Do you get to play like that very often?"

"Mm, not really. But that's okay. Ma needs my help." Nathan's blue eyes were so serious.

"I'm sure it's been hard for you since your pa died. You've had to become the man of the family." The boy shrugged. "Well, I think you've done a fine job. I can tell your ma relies on you a lot."

"Yeah." He paused as if he was thinking. "Can I tell you a secret?"

"Sure." What kind of secret could an eight-year-old have?

"Ma said Pa had an accident." He stole a glance around for anyone listening. "But I know he ran off," he finished in a whisper.

"Ran off? What makes you think so?"

"I heard Uncle Phillip and Aunt Grace talking about it once. They didn't know I was listening."

"Who are Uncle Phillip and Aunt Grace?"

"Aunt Grace is Ma's sister. They used to live down the road."

"I see. Well, what did they say?"

"They said it was too bad Pa got mixed up with some outlaws and if he didn't rob a bank, he'd still be alive."

"Did they say how he died?"

"In a gunfight with the sheriff." Nathan's eyes bulged as he leaned forward.

"Are you sure you heard right?"

"Yeah, I was outside the door."

"Did you tell Abigail and Emily what you heard?"

"Nah, they're too little." He looked around again. "And don't tell Ma!" His eyes narrowed and he shook his finger in Travis' face.

"Why not?"

"She doesn't know. She still thinks Pa had an accident."

Travis almost choked on the lump in his throat. "You really are the man of the family."

"I guess so." Nathan shrugged and removed his wet shirt. "Hey, do you think we could do the three-legged race at the town picnic?"

"Uh... Town picnic?" A man could have lost his hat on that turn. Amazing how a child's mind worked. "When is it?"

"I don't know for sure, but it's real soon. Will you do it with me?"

"Well now, I think this leg of mine is almost as good as new. I think I could manage that, as long as you don't outrun me."

Chapter Sixteen

Carrie handed Travis a glass of cider. He smiled and nodded, but she avoided his gaze. Would the fire in her cheeks betray her? Would he even notice? Like she had noticed the strength of his arms around her before? Like she noticed how he smelled? Of work and sweat, and manliness.

"Travis and me are gonna win the three-legged race at the town picnic this year." Nathan smiled and licked cider from his upper lip.

"Nathan…" She shook her head and waved him off.

"When is the picnic?" Travis took another sip of cider.

"Next Saturday."

"Well, we're going to make quite a team." Travis smiled as Nathan beamed up at him.

"Just don't get your heart set on winning, son. There can only be one winner. The point is to enjoy the competition." Carried looked Nathan in the eye.

"There's no harm in dreaming, is there?" Travis gave her an impish grin.

"Hello!" A woman's voice grabbed their attention.

They turned to see a man and woman with a wagon full of children pulling up in front of the barn.

Carrie sighed. The Shafers. Oh, fine. Well, at least she didn't have to answer Travis' question. She walked over to greet them as the children spilled out of the wagon. "Hello. This is a surprise." She never liked surprises.

"Yes, we thought we'd stop by on our way back from town. We just wanted to look in on you and see how the crops are coming along." Esther straightened her skirt and bonnet.

Carrie frowned and bit the inside of her lip. Look in on them? Ha! She wanted a look at Travis McCallister. Wanted to see for herself if there was anything indecent going on at the Lindquist's. Carrie snorted under her breath. She enjoyed disappointing the old busybody.

"Hey, Josiah!" Nathan hollered and waved. He ran toward the children with Abigail and Emily on his heels.

"Martha, Martha!" Abigail hugged the visitor.

"Ma, can we go play?" Nathan asked poised to run.

"Yes. Just be careful."

The young brood dashed off in search of adventure.

"Don't go too far," Lemuel Shafer called after them. "Caleb, keep an eye on the younger ones."

"Hello, Lemuel." Travis shook the man's hand. "How are you?"

"Fit as a fiddle. I noticed the way you're watering the crops. I'd like to see it."

"I'd be happy to show it to you." Travis led the way toward the field beyond the barn.

"Does it work?"

"It's been working fine."

"If it works like you say it does, I may have to start doing it at my place."

Esther and Leah looked at Carrie. There was nothing to do but invite them in the house. "Would you like some coffee or cider?"

"Sure. Those two will be gone for a while, if I know men." Esther chuckled and waved her arm. "It'll give us a chance to catch up. Come along, Leah." The girl followed her mother without a word.

Catch up? That was the last thing Carrie wanted to do with Esther Shafer. Travis had better hurry.

"So, would you like coffee, or cider?" Carrie repeated her question.

"Oh, coffee, please." Esther lowered herself into a chair with a groan.

"May I have some cider?" Leah spoke for the first time.

"Of course." Carrie poured two cups of coffee and a glass of cider and set them on the table, along with fresh bread and jam.

"How has your family been?" Esther wasted no time starting the conversation.

Carrie took a long sip from her cup and set it on the table. "Fine. And how are all of you?" Not that she wanted to know. But she had been taught to mind her manners.

"Oh, we're doing well. The kids are all growing like weeds. Josiah's big enough now to really be of help to his pa. Caleb sure is glad of that. And little Amos tries to keep up with his brothers." Esther laughed and spread jam on a slice of bread.

A smile crossed Carrie's lips. She pictured Emily's brown curls bobbing in the wind as she ran after Nathan and Abigail. Her little legs struggling to catch up.

"Did you know Leah wants to be a teacher?"

"No, I didn't know that. Do you like children?" Carrie looked at the girl. She seemed afraid of her own shadow. How would she ever face a school room full of rambunctious students?

"Yes, I do. I…" Leah began to answer.

"My land, she loves children, and they adore her. We can't go anywhere but they don't swarm around her like bees. She just attracts the little ones."

"I'm sure you'll be a good teacher, then." Carrie wasn't at all sure.

"I hope so," Leah answered for herself.

"Leah is a big help with the little ones at home. Keeping them out from underfoot. Still, that Martha is my precious baby."

So, the youngest was Martha. Carrie had forgotten her name. "Well, I'm glad your family is well."

"Oh yes. And how is your little family doing? I see the children are getting big. I can't believe Emily. I almost didn't recognize her, she's grown so much since I saw her last. What is she, four now?"

"She will be soon." How did Esther Shafer even know that?

"And Abigail is what, six?"

"Five."

"That's right. And Nathan's the same age as my Josiah. Emily and Martha should get together more often. They'd be great playmates. In fact, all of our children should have the chance to be together more. Maybe we should have your three over soon for the day."

"I… don't know… I…"

"Oh, they'd love it. You saw how they all took up with each other when we got here. The more the merrier, I always say." The jovial woman laughed and spread jam on another piece of bread. "This jam is delicious."

"Thank you."

"It really is. Chokecherry?"

"Yes."

"I can never get my chokecherry to come out right, so I quit trying." Esther waved her hand in defeat.

"Do you like to cook, Leah?" Carrie addressed the silent girl again.

"Yes, I do. I help Ma with the cooking and the baking."

"She's going to make some lucky young man a good wife one of these days," her mother interrupted again.

If Leah ever got a marriage proposal, her mother would accept before the girl had a chance.

The door burst open, and rowdy children spilled into the room. "Ma, can we go to the swimming hole? It's really hot." Nathan stopped in front of Carrie, gasping for breath.

"Nathan! You know you don't come into the house that way, and you're interrupting." Not that Esther Shafer would notice.

"I'm sorry. But can we?"

"No. You need someone to go with you, and everyone is busy. And I don't think the Shafers are going to be here long enough to go swimming." The children groaned in unison.

"Leah could take them." Esther looked at her eldest, who didn't respond.

Carrie had a better idea. "If you are all hot and tired, why don't you go to the barn and play with the kittens?"

"You have kittens?" Caleb clapped his hands.

"Yeah, you wanna see 'em?" Abigail wiped her face with her hands.

"Sure!" The eager bunch ran through the kitchen door, colliding with Travis and Lemuel.

"Whoa! What's your hurry?" Travis caught Amos as he tripped and almost fell.

"We gotta show them the kittens," Nathan called over his shoulder.

"Don't go far. We're leaving soon," Lemuel called after the children.

"Well, did you see the irrigation, Lem?" Esther shoved the last bite of bread in her mouth.

"I sure did, and it's a wonder. I've heard tell of it but never seen it. Travis is going to help dig one at our place."

"Well, isn't that nice. See, Carrie, the children will have to come over soon." Esther nodded and winked.

"We better get home, Ma. It's getting late, and chores are waiting." Lemuel shook hands with Travis. "Thank you for showing me around."

"You're welcome. I'll be at your place Thursday." He and Carrie followed the Shafers outside.

"See you then." The slight man let out an ear-splitting whistle, which brought the four youngest of his brood running.

"Say goodbye. It's time for us to be getting home." Esther clambered into the wagon, with much effort. "Thank you for the hospitality. We've been long overdue for a visit."

"You're welcome."

The children waved and hollered their goodbyes as the wagon pulled onto the road.

Travis smiled and looked at Carrie. "That was a nice surprise."

She just looked at him.

"Wasn't it?"

She sighed and shook her head. "That Esther Shafer, she is something."

He chuckled. "She does like the sound of her own voice, doesn't she?"

"You could say that." Carrie smirked and shrugged. And to do all the talking.

"But they are nice people."

"I suppose so."

Chapter Seventeen

"Well, I better start supper." Carrie started toward the house.

"Carrie, could I speak to you first?"

"Can it wait?"

"No."

Carrie stared at Travis for a moment. His face was so serious. What was so important that he had to talk to her right now?

"Nathan, can you help your sisters wash up, please?"

"Yes, Ma." He took Emily's hand. "Come on, Abby."

"Thank you." She turned her attention back to Travis and put her hands on her hips. "What is it?"

"Um, come with me." Taking hold of her arm, he guided her into the barn.

She turned and crossed her arms. "What is it? What is so important and secretive that you have to usher me in here?"

"I spoke with Nathan earlier, here in the barn."

Carrie stared with crossed arms.

"He knows what happened to his father."

Carrie stiffened and her head tilted. "He knows?

Everything?"

Travis nodded.

Her eyes narrowed to slits and she hissed. "You told him about Peter? How could you? I told you not to say anything."

Travis held up his hands to quiet her. "I didn't tell him. He already knew."

"How could he have known?"

"He said he overheard his aunt and uncle talking about it a while back."

"Grace and Phillip?" she asked. Travis nodded again. "I don't believe it. They never would have told him about Peter."

"I doubt they meant for him to hear."

"But... when did... I..." Carrie's mind spun like a top.

"I'm sorry, but I thought you should know."

Carrie stared at the floor for a moment before looking up at Travis. "What else did he say? Did he tell Abby and Emmy?"

"No. He said they were too young to understand. And he said that I shouldn't tell you, because you still think his pa died in an accident."

"Oh my..." She turned away and stared up at the sun peeking through the cracks in the roof. She wiped the tears running down her cheeks and whirled back around. "What do

I do now? How do I explain to him? What do I say?"

"You need to pray for God to give you the right words."

"Why? What does God care about me or my children?" she scoffed, with one hand on her hip and taking a swipe at another tear with the other.

"God loves you, Carrie, and He loves your children."

"Ha! I don't believe that. If God loved me, why did He take my husband from me? Why did He leave three children without their father?" She stomped her foot on the dirt floor.

"God didn't take your husband from you, Carrie. That was a direct consequence of Peter's actions, not God's."

Her eyes flashed as she clenched her teeth. "God betrayed me!"

Travis lowered his voice. "No, God didn't betray you, Carrie. Peter did. All this time you've been blaming God, when Peter was at fault. I know it's a hard thing to hear. But you need to accept the truth. And then you need to forgive Peter, and God. And most of all, you need to let the Lord into your life, because He really does love you."

"I don't believe you!"

"That doesn't change the fact that He is God, and He loves you and your children."

He might as well have slapped her across the face. Peter's fault? Forgive God? It couldn't be true. Blinded by tears, she found the door and ran from the barn.

"All right, children, pick up your things. It's time for bed." Carrie put away the last of the supper dishes.

"Ma, can't we stay up just a little longer? Travis said he'd tell us a story," Nathan entreated.

"Yeah, Mama, Tavis gonna tell us a story," Emily added.

"Not tonight. Maybe tomorrow." The children moaned.

"Hey, if you go on to bed like your Ma says, tomorrow I'll tell you a really long story," Travis promised them. They hurried to do as they were told.

"You don't have to bribe them, you know. I expect them to obey without bribery."

"I'm sorry. I was just trying to help. I didn't mean to interfere."

"I know." She gave a half-hearted smile. "Just don't make a habit of it."

He raised his right hand. "I promise. Well, I better head to the barn myself." He drained his coffee cup.

"Really? It's early."

"I have some things to do before bed."

"Oh. Well, good night, then."

"Good night." He closed the kitchen door behind him.

Carrie's hand closed on the knob of Nathan's bedroom door. She took a deep breath and closed her eyes before tapping on the door. "Nathan?"

"Yeah, Ma?" he answered, as she opened the door.

"I thought you might be asleep already."

"No." He slipped his night shirt over his head. "I was just thinking. Me and Travis... I mean, we need to practice for the three-legged race. I really want to beat that old Bert and Willie Thompson this year." He pounded his fist in his hand as he plopped on his bed. "They think they're so smart."

Carrie smiled at his youthful enthusiasm. "Nate, I want to talk to you for a minute."

"Did I do something wrong?"

"Oh. No. Nothing like that." She sat next to him on the bed. "Travis said that you told him you know what happened to your pa."

He sat upright. "I told him not to tell you! That was s'posed to be our secret." He dropped his head and pouted.

"It's all right." She cupped his chin in her hand. "Don't be

angry with Travis. He told me because he's worried about you."
The boy dropped his head again. "Nathan, look at me... please."
Carrie waited for him to look up. "I know about your father.
I've always known. But I didn't tell you and your sisters because
I thought you were too young to understand. And I didn't want
you to think less of him. I am so sorry that you had to find out
from Aunt Grace and Uncle Phillip."

He shrugged. "It's okay."

"No, it isn't. That is a very hard thing to hear, especially that
way." She wrapped him in her arms. "I guess I should have told
you. I should have known that you were man enough to handle
it." She kissed his head as he laid it against her shoulder. She
choked back more tears as she whispered. "I am so proud of
you for trying to protect me. And Abigail and Emily."

They sat in silence for a moment before Nathan spoke.
"Ma?"

"Hmm?"

"Was Pa a bad man?"

"No, Nathan. Your father was not a bad man. He was a
good man, and he loved us very much. Even though he made
some bad decisions, he did so because he loved us."

"Sometimes I still miss him."

"So do I, Sweetheart. So do I." She hugged him tighter. "Well, it's getting late. You best get into bed."

He crawled under the sheet. "Ma?"

"What?"

"Do you like Travis?"

"Yes, I do. Do you?" She tucked in his covers.

"Uh huh. I sure hope we win the three-legged race." Carrie smiled and kissed his forehead.

"Good night. Sleep tight."

"Nite, Ma."

Carrie blew out the lamp and closed the door behind her. When had her little boy become a man? Peter would be so proud.

Chapter Eighteen

"Ma, did we bring my hoop?" Abigail asked from the back of the wagon, for the third time.

"Yes Abby. It's under the picnic basket." Carrie nodded and reassured her again.

"The hoop race is for sissies. The three-legged race is tougher. Huh, Travis?"

"Well, the three-legged race is tough, for sure. But I don't think I'd be any good at rolling a hoop with nothing but a stick."

"See." Abigail stuck her tongue out at her brother.

"Well, we'll see who wins," Nathan sparred back.

"All right, that's enough. I know you'll both do your best."

"To tell the truth, I'm kind of looking forward to the tug-of-war," Travis confided to Carrie. "I hear it's a real contest." He guided the wagon to a stop.

"Oh, there's Grace and Phillip!" Carrie waved as the three children jumped up and down in the wagon. "Hello!"

"Carrie! Carrie!" A woman who looked almost just like Carrie, but with blond hair, ran around to her side of the wagon. Carrie climbed down and hugged her tight.

"It's so good to see you. Grace and Phillip, I want you to meet Travis McCallister." Carrie pointed in his direction. "And these are their children, Ruth, Levi, Sarah, and Simon."

"Hello," Grace smiled.

"Phillip Baxter. Pleasure to meet you." Phillip shook Travis' hand.

"We're so glad to meet you. We've heard about the handsome farmhand staying at the Lindquist farm. You're quite the mystery man." Grace laughed and lifted a basket from their wagon.

Travis blushed and grinned. "Oh, there's no mystery here, I can guarantee you."

"How in the world did you hear about Travis over in Red Dale?" Carrie stopped in mid-motion with her hand on a wooden box.

"From several people. You know how gossip travels." Grace waved it off with her hand.

"All too well." She could thank Virginia Lambert or Esther Shafer, no doubt. Why couldn't people mind their own business?

"Uncle Phillip, I'm gonna be in the hoop race!" Abigail

stood tall and pointed her thumb at her chest.

Phillip chuckled as he lifted her from the wagon. "Are you? Sarah is, too. She's been practicing all week."

"Travis and I are going to win the three-legged race!" Nathan bragged.

"Well, I don't know about that. But we're going to give it our best shot, that's for sure." Travis offered an encouraging smile to his young partner.

"Good. Levi and I are going to team up for that, and I think Aunt Grace and Ruthie are, too. But I'm looking forward to the tug-of-war." Phillip rubbed his hands together.

"I've heard stories about that." Travis adjusted his hat.

"Oh, it's something to behold," Grace interjected, giggling. "Especially the year Henry Fredricks ended up head first in the mud on top of Mitch Watkins."

"Oh, I remember that." Grace and Phillip laughed out loud.

"What happened?" Travis looked from one to the other.

"Well, Henry Fredricks is a rather... large man..." Carrie held her hands out, about the width of Henry's shoulders.

"And Mitch Watkins is a twig. He weighs about a hundred and ten pounds soaking wet, with his clothes on," Phillip finished between gasps of air.

"Hopefully, this year will be as exciting. I'm really looking forward to it now!" Travis rubbed his hands together.

"Hello, Carrie."

Carrie turned to face Frank Robinson. "Oh, hello, Frank." Oh, fine. Another busybody.

"I was wondering if I could persuade you to join me for lunch?"

His toothy grin through his thick black mustache turned her stomach. Have lunch with him? She'd rather eat with a snake.

"No, thank you. My sister's family is here, and we are all going to eat together."

"I see. Well, do you mind if I join all of you?"

Of all the… He was determined, if nothing else. What could she say? To refuse would be rude. Good manners always won out over personal feelings. "Oh. All right. You're welcome to join us." Disgust tinged her voice, and she didn't care.

Travis studied Frank Robinson from his seat on the grass under a big cottonwood. Frank's cap was set for Carrie. Anyone could see that. But anyone could also see that Carrie didn't want anything to do with him. Anyone but Frank Robinson.

Travis almost felt sorry for him. Almost.

"So, Frank, what do you do? For a living, I mean?" Travis tried to make conversation.

"I run the freight office."

"You run it. So, you've worked your way up. That's very commendable."

"No. My father started it over twenty years ago. I took over when he went to glory." Frank sounded defensive.

"I remember your father. He was a good man. You could always depend on him to give you a fair deal on shipping your crops to market." Phillip jumped into the conversation.

"Well, I hope you think you still get a fair deal." Frank seemed defensive.

"Oh, of course. I just meant that your father was a good man."

"How is your mother doing?" Grace interjected, with a glance at her husband.

"She's getting by. She hasn't been doing very well since father passed on."

"She didn't feel like coming today?" Grace continued the questions.

"No, she doesn't get out much anymore."

"That's too bad. Tell her we missed her. We should stop by the next time we're in Cedar Creek."

"I'm sure she'd like that. She does get lonely, I think, with just me for company."

Frank Robinson wasn't such a bad fellow. But Travis didn't trust the man. Maybe it was because he had his eye on Carrie. Maybe not. Travis couldn't nail it down, yet.

"May we go?" Ruth put her hand on her mother's shoulder and leaned in.

"Have you finished eating?" Several small heads nodded. "Ask your Pa, then."

All eyes turned to Phillip. "Well, it's all right with me. But you better ask Aunt Carrie."

With so many expectant little faces staring at her, Carrie tried not to giggle. "I don't know. I think there's a special rule that you have to wait for twenty minutes before you can play."

"Ma!" Nathan groaned.

"No. No. It's a special picnic rule." Carrie raised her eyebrows and shook her head.

"Yeah. I've heard about that rule." Travis sat up straight and nodded. "Makes good sense to me, too. I couldn't run right now if I tried." He winked at Carrie.

The adults erupted in laughter. "Of course, you can go. Go. Have fun, but don't go too far, because the events will be starting soon." Phillip released the gleeful youngsters. The children scampered off with peals of laughter.

Grace grabbed Simon before he could wander very far. "Oh, no you don't. You're staying with me."

"Oh," Phillip moaned, and rubbed his stomach. "I ate too much. It's just going to weigh me down during the tug-of-war."

"Maybe we should tell the judge that your team may have an unfair advantage, with you and Travis and your full stomachs." Grace poked her husband's swollen belly.

Phillip smiled and winked as he lay back on the grass.

"We'll take all the advantage we can get." Travis leaned back against the trunk of the big cottonwood.

"Just be glad you're not entered in the pie eating contest," Carrie teased her brother-in-law. Phillip and Travis groaned and rolled their eyes.

"Maybe the raw egg relay would be just what you need," Grace goaded them.

"Stop. Stop, or I will be sick." Phillip held his stomach and groaned.

Chapter Nineteen

"Ma!" Nathan called. "It's time for the hoop race. Hurry!"

The adults scrambled to their feet, grabbed the girls' hoops, and hurried to the first contest. The contestants lined up at the starting line, hoops and sticks at the ready. The school teacher, Ralph Matthews, held up a flag. "Ready, set, *go!*"

They were off, on the first of three laps. The racers were clustered together, rounding the first turn.

"Go, Abby!" Carrie screamed and waved.

"Hooray, Abby!" Travis echoed in her ear.

"Sarah, Sarah, Sarah!" Grace and Phillip chanted together.

The crowd cheered, and the runners kept spinning their hoops. Sarah and Abigail caught up with the leader and were tied for second.

"Yeah, Abby!"

"Go, Sarah!"

"Ohhhh!" The crowd gasped in unison.

Abigail's and Sarah's hoops collided with another girl trying to pass them. The three contenders landed in the dust, and their hoops spun away. Olivia Matthews flew by them and finished in first place.

Abigail sat in the dust and burst into tears. Carrie knelt beside her and wiped her face. "You did such a good job. I had no idea you could spin a hoop so well. You almost won."

"But I didn't win!" And there came a new gush of tears.

Carrie pulled her close. "I know. I know. But you did your best, and that's all you can do."

Sarah knelt down by her cousin. "I'm sorry, Abby. That darned old Tessa Davis. She got in my way, and then I got in your way. I'm sorry. I didn't mean to make you fall."

Abigail sniffed and looked up at her cousin through tear-stained eyelashes. "Thanks, Sarah."

Sarah gave her a quick hug. "I gotta find my folks." She jumped up and ran into Travis.

"Whoa."

"Sorry. I'm looking for my Mama and Papa."

"They're right over there." Travis pointed them out, and Sarah ran toward them. "Well, now, Miss Abby, that was quite a race. You are some hoop spinner." He knelt on one knee next to the girl and Carrie.

Abigail just glared up at him through her eyelashes.

Travis looked at Carrie, who shrugged. "Hey, I could use

some help getting ready for the tug-of-war. I need to warm up, and Nathan's busy. Would you help me?" He offered his hand.

She looked at him and sniffed. Not at all sure, she took his hand.

"There you go. Stand up and dust yourself off. That's about the only thing you can do when you take a tumble. That's a girl. All right. The tug-of-war's this way."

"But the three-legged race is next!" Nathan overheard the conversation.

"I know. I'll be there," Travis assured him. His work-roughened hand all but swallowed Abigail's little one as they walked together.

Carrie breathed a sigh of relief. Travis had such a way with the children. And it was good for them to have a man's influence again, even if it was only for a little while.

Nathan was right. The three-legged race was the next event. With young Simon in her arms and Emily by the hand, Carrie led the way to the front of the crowd. "Can you see from here?" she checked with Abigail and Sarah. They nodded their answer.

Phillip and Levi, and Grace and Ruth were ready to go. Travis and Nathan stood tied together. Travis secured the knot on their rope as Nathan glowered at Bert and Willie Thompson. Willie sneered back before Bert jostled him off balance.

"There's Mama and Papa!" Sarah waved to Phillip and Grace.

"And there's Tavis." Emily clapped her hands. "Hi, Tavis."

"He can't hear you, Emmy," Abigail scolded her sister.

"Abby, it doesn't matter." Carrie held up her hand to shield her eyes from the sun.

"Hello, Carrie."

Carrie jumped at the voice in her ear and glanced to her left. "Hello, Esther." What did she want now?

"Fine day for a picnic, isn't it?"

"Yes, it is." Carrie watched the starting line.

"Josiah and Caleb are entered in this race. I see Nathan is racing with Travis."

"Yes, he is."

"Isn't that your sister? Grace? And her husband, Phillip? Is that Caleb and Ruth? My, they're growing so fast."

Would this woman be quiet? They were going to miss the race if she didn't shut up. "Yes, they are."

The starting gun sounded. The crowd cheered for their favorites as the teams made their way down the course. Phillip and Levi were the first to fall, and then Grace and Ruth tumbled. Next, Josiah and Caleb Shafer went down. Then all teams were back on their feet and racing again.

"Go, Nate! Go, Travis!" Carrie pumped her arm up and down until she caught Esther Shafer's accusing look out of the corner of her eye. "Come on, Grace and Ruthie! Run, Phillip! Run, Levi!"

But Grace and Ruth tripped each other and fell again. Levi couldn't keep up with Phillip, and they went down hard. The crowd moaned.

"Go!" Carrie tried not to scream in Simon's ear.

"Come on, Josiah. Come on, Caleb," Esther cheered for her boys.

Travis and Nathan had a good stride going, until Nathan tripped and almost collapsed. Travis held him up with both arms until he was back on his feet. They recovered in time to cross the finish line just ahead of Bert and Willie Thompson.

"Travis and Nate won, Mama!" Abigail swung Emily in a circle. "Yeah!"

"Indeed, they did, Abby. Let's go congratulate them." Carrie grabbed Emily's hand and led the way to the winners.

Jack Dawson pinned blue ribbons on Travis and Nathan

and declared them the winners. Travis lifted the boy up in his big arms and swung him around as he yelped with delight.

Nathan was so happy. So proud. Carrie's heart smiled to see his joy. It had been way too long.

"We won! We won!" Nathan yelled at the top of his lungs.

"We sure did," Travis laughed and shared in the victory.

"I knew we would. I just knew it."

"Well, I'm glad you had confidence in us."

"Ha, ha. We beat Bert and Willie! Whoo!"

"Yes, we did. But it's important to be a good winner," Travis warned him.

"What do you mean?"

"Well, a good loser doesn't pout or lay blame on someone else, right?" Nathan nodded his agreement. "Well, a good winner doesn't gloat or show off in front of the other contestants."

"Not even a little?" Nathan scrunched his face.

"Not even a little. But it doesn't mean you can't be proud of yourself and celebrate, either."

"Okay!" Nathan jumped back into Travis' arms and wrapped his arms around the man's neck. "Thank you, Travis," he whispered in his ear.

"You're welcome, Nate."

"Ladies and gentlemen. This is the final event of the day. The tug-of-war," Reverend Chandler announced, loud and clear. "We have the red team and the blue team. The green bandana marks the middle of the rope. The object is to pull the scarf to your team's side of the mud pit. The first team to do so is the winner. Pick your sides, gentlemen."

"Do you like red, or blue?" Phillip scanned the men lining up on both sides of the rope.

"I guess the blue team looks good, eh? Who's that big man up front?" Travis nodded toward their self-appointed leader.

"Oh, that's Zeb Thompson. He runs the feed and seed."

"Thompson. Does he have two boys named, uh, Bert and Willie?"

"I think so. Why?"

"Nathan was ecstatic that we beat them in the three-legged race. You know boys."

Phillip nodded. "Oh, terrific. Mitch Watkins is on our team. We're going to have to do double duty."

"I'm ready if you are." Travis wrapped the rope around his wrists and nodded to Phillip.

"You could lose a hand that way." Phillip looked worried.

"Hasn't happened yet." Travis spread his feet and bent his knees. "Extra leverage. Extra advantage."

"Well, I'll do it my way." Phillip spread his hands apart and gripped the rope. "Hmm, Frank Robinson is leading the red team. You suppose he's trying to prove something?"

Travis dug his feet into the grass. "Like what?"

Phillip sighed and shook his head. "Never mind." He squatted and hunkered into position.

"Ready?" Reverend Chandler held up the starting pistol. The teams nodded in unison. "Go!" He fired the gun.

Travis gritted his teeth and pulled. "Pull, Phillip!" he ordered. Phillip grunted in his ear.

"Pull, pull, pull!" the blue team leader yelled in rhythm.

Travis' muscles bulged each time he yanked the rope. Tug-of-war should have been called tug-of-sod. Gain two inches. Lose three. This could be a long battle. The rope bit into Travis' wrists through his sleeves, and his thighs were on fire. But the blue team had to hold their ground.

"That's it! The kerchief's on our side." Zeb Thompson stood up and claimed victory. "We won!"

Reverend Chandler examined the bandana. "Well, it's on

the edge, but not quite all the way over on your side."

"What? No. You said…."

"Pull!" Frank Robinson shouted to his team. The line of men behind him heaved in unison with one big jerk of the rope.

The blue team flew like frightened birds. Mitch Watkins flopped in the mud, again, followed by Zeb Thompson.

Phillip helped Travis off the ground, but a staggering teammate knocked him off balance. He lurched forward still holding Travis' arm.

"Whoa! Whoa!" Splash!

Travis pulled his head out of the brown muck. "Phillip?" He swiped his hands down the length of his face.

Phillip sat up, wiping mud from his eyes. "What?"

"Do you see what I see?"

Phillip squinted and looked up. "I sure do."

Frank Robinson stood at the edge of the mud hole, as clean and shiny as a new penny, laughing. "Too bad, fellas. Better luck next year."

That was it. Frank Robinson had just played his last card and lost. Travis and Phillip laid their sludge covered hands on his clean shirt sleeves.

"What are you doing? Come on, fellas. It was just a joke."

"So is this."

Travis and Phillip flung Frank like a rock in a sling shot. He sprawled in the middle of the muck, face down, and came up spewing mud.

Phillip slapped Travis on the back. "Now that's funny."

Chapter Twenty

"I'm sorry; I did the best I could." Phillip swiped muddy water from his shirt. "The water was almost as muddy was we were."

"Thank goodness I brought an extra shirt." Grace handed him the spare. "I have another one if you want to borrow it, Travis."

"I think I'll be all right. We don't have as far to get home as you do. Thank you, though." Travis put his hat over his mud caked hair.

"Mama, can Sarah come home with us?" Abigail asked her mother. "Please?"

"Oh, I don't know. It's been a big day, and everyone is pretty tired. I think it would be better another time."

"But, Ma…" Nathan begged.

"I have an idea. Why don't you three come with us, instead?" Grace suggested. "It's been quite a while since you've been to our house, and we'd love to have you."

"Oh, Grace. You don't have to do that. I…"

"I know I don't have to. I want to. My children have been

pestering me to have their cousins come for a visit anyway. Phillip doesn't mind, do you dear?" She gave him sideways glance. "Besides, then you can have a little peace and quiet."

"Well…"

"I think it's a fine idea." Phillip placed a box in their wagon. "Well, Miss Emily, how would you like to spend some time at my house?" He scooped his niece up in his arms, and she giggled.

"Well, I guess it's all settled, then. Children, help me pack up our things so we can go home and get you ready."

"Don't worry about all of that. You go on ahead and get them ready. We'll finish up here and bring your things and pick up the children." Grace shooed her sister toward her own wagon.

"Are you sure? I feel guilty leaving you with all of this work."

"Nonsense. It isn't that much, and it will give you enough time to do what you need to do."

"All right. You win. I'll go. We'll see you soon." She called to her children over her shoulder. "Nathan, Abigail, Emily, come on. You need to get ready to go to Aunt Grace's." The Lindquist children jumped into the wagon, and Carrie settled into her seat. Travis clicked the team into motion.

"Grace, are you sure about this? I don't want you to think

that you have to do this." Carrie scanned the room. "Oh, Emmy's doll. She can't sleep without this." She tucked it into the carpetbag. "You know I'd be glad for your children to spend time with us, just… not today." She gave a weak smile.

"Carrie, you've always been such a worrywart. Ma said you started worrying about me the day I was born." She grabbed her big sister's hand. "If I didn't want to do this, I wouldn't have mentioned it. With four of our own, it really is no bother to add a few more. Besides, they can entertain each other, and I can finish the curtains for Ruth and Sarah's room. It'll be fine. They enjoy being together so much. And they don't get to see each other since we moved to Red Dale." She rubbed Carrie's arm.

"Well, thank you. And make sure they mind you and Phillip. I don't want them behaving like hooligans while they're gone. They know better."

"They'll be fine. You be sure to get some rest. You need to take better care of yourself, you know."

"Now who's worrying?"

"We better get going, Grace," Phillip called from the wagon seat. "If you two keep talking, it'll be dark before we get home."

"All right." Grace led the way outside and gave Carrie a

quick hug. "I love you."

"I love you, too. Thank you again."

Grace climbed aboard and settled herself next to her husband. Phillip clucked to the horses, and they were off.

"Bye, Ma. Take care of Chester." Nathan waved with both arms.

"Bye, Mama." The girls waved too.

She waved back. "Goodbye. Behave yourselves and mind your manners. I love you."

Chapter Twenty-One

Carrie woke with a start and sat up on the side of the bed. The house was so quiet. Too quiet. What was that noise? Someone was in the kitchen. But who? She slipped into her robe and opened her bedroom door.

"Good morning."

Travis turned from the stove. "I'm sorry. Did I wake you? I burned my hand on the blasted stove and dropped the cover. I was trying to be quiet. Honest." He gave her a sheepish grin.

Carrie stopped mid-step. She rubbed her eyes and stared. "What's that?" There, in the middle of the kitchen table, sat her mother's teapot. She ran and lifted it in the air.

"Where did this come from? What's it doing here?" Was it her mother's? It was! "I don't understand. I s…"

"Sold it," Travis finished her sentence.

She clutched the teapot to her body. "How did you know?"

"I saw it in Dawson's store. Jack Dawson said you sold it to him just about the time the bank loan was due."

How did he find out? Did Mr. Dawson tell him? How did he get it back?

"Jack promised to hold it until I could buy it back for you."

"How did you pay for it?"

"Lemuel Shafer gave me a little money for digging his irrigation." He studied her face. "So, I guess the Shafers are your friends after all."

Tears dripped onto her prized possession. "Oh, Travis. I don't know what to say." She lifted her head. "Except that you didn't have to do that."

"I know. But I figured you've sacrificed enough. You shouldn't have to give up your only heirloom, too." He smiled and tilted his head.

"Thank you so much. I can't believe it! I thought it was gone forever." She ran over and flung her arm around Travis' shoulders.

He patted her hand. "You're welcome. I know how much it means to you."

Carrie placed the pot back in its place on the sideboard. "There. Back where you belong." She had missed that teapot so much. She didn't know how much until that moment.

"Much better. Can I get you some breakfast? I'm frying

potatoes, and I was just going to scramble some eggs."

"You're cooking? Why?"

"Well, I *was* going to fend for myself and let you sleep in. And then I was going to get after the chores."

"Oh."

"Would you like some potatoes and eggs?" He repeated his question.

"Sounds good. I'll get dressed and help you." He shouldn't be cooking her breakfast. She needed to hurry.

"No need to hurry. I'm not a bad cook, if I do say so myself. Of course, I may be a little partial." He winked and smiled.

"Well, you look fresh as a daisy." Travis poured Carrie a cup of coffee. "Are you hungry?"

"Mm-hmm." She took the cup and sipped the coffee.

"Well, then have a seat, ma'am. Breakfast is served." He dished up the food and set a plate in front of her and one across the table. "I hope you like it. There isn't much can go wrong with potatoes and eggs."

Carrie sampled her breakfast. "Mmm. You are a good cook."

"Don't judge too quick. It's only breakfast," he chuckled. "It's nice to cook for someone besides myself for a change." So nice. So nice not to have to eat alone, too.

"I think it would be lonely, just travelling from place to place."

"I do get tired of my own company sometimes." But the Lord was good company.

"Do you have any family?"

"A brother and two sisters."

"Are they in Pennsylvania?"

He looked up from his plate. "They were, last I knew." He hadn't thought about his family in a long time. Not even Elizabeth. That old ache flared in his gut.

"You're not sure?"

"I haven't kept in touch with them since I left. It's hard to get mail when you move around."

"Do you miss them?"

He shrugged. "I've gotten so used to being alone that I forget I have family." He took a bite of his food. It was time to change the subject. "What about you? Do you have any family other than Grace?"

She stopped with her fork in mid-air. "No. Our parents have passed on. We have… had a younger brother, Daniel. He was younger than Grace. He died when we were young."

He laid his fork on his plate. "What happened?"

"He was trampled by horses." Carrie's face clouded over.

"I'm sorry. I didn't mean to upset you."

"I just haven't thought about it for a while." Her eyes filled with tears, and the cloud on her face turned darker. One tear slipped down her cheek, unnoticed.

"Carrie?" Travis whispered her name.

She stared at him but didn't see him.

"Are you all right?"

"I haven't thought about Daniel in a long time."

"I am so sorry. I didn't mean to dredge up painful memories." How could he have caused her more pain? She'd had enough. He reached across the table and took hold of her hand. She didn't notice.

She sat across from him but was miles away. "It was my fault. We had gone to town, and Pa asked me to bring the buggy to the bank. I went to get it and Daniel wanted to come with me."

"Everything was fine until someone shot off a gun in the street. The horses spooked and took off like they had fire under their tails. It seemed like they galloped for miles, and then the back wheel hit a rock. The buggy jumped up and Daniel was thrown forward, under the horses. I got him back to town as fast as I could, but..." She shrugged and shook her head. "It was too late."

"It was a horrible accident. You can't blame yourself."

She scraped the table with her thumbnail. "That's what my folks said. I remember Ma said it was just Daniel's time to go home to be with the Lord."

"They were right."

"Why'd he have to die so young? He was only eight. Why didn't God take me? I was the oldest."

"God tells us that His ways are not our ways. But He always has a plan, and it's always for our ultimate good. And what could be better for Daniel than to be in paradise, where there's no pain or sorrow? All he knows is peace and joy."

Silence surrounded them. Travis refilled their coffee cups and set the pot on the table. He leaned his elbows on the table and laid his head on his hands. *Dear Lord, please lift Carrie's sorrow and show her Your joy. Help her to see the truth.*

Chapter Twenty-Two

"Are you ready to go?" Travis tightened the rope on the tarp.

"Almost. I just have to get the preserves I forgot to give Grace when she was here."

Carrie hurried back into the house to retrieve the promised blackberry preserves. "Okay. I'm ready." She closed the door behind her.

They climbed into the wagon and settled themselves in the seat as Chester barked and tried to jump into the wagon. "No, Chester. You have to stay here. And be good."

"How far is it to your sister's?"

"About two hours, in good weather."

"Well, I guess we better get ready for a long ride." Travis released the wagon brake and clucked to the team. The wagon lurched forward.

"I hope Grace hasn't had any trouble with my children being there. She already has her hands full."

"I'm sure everything's fine." Travis leaned his elbows on his knees. "You might as well enjoy the trip. It's going to be the last bit of peace and quiet you'll have for a while."

Carrie removed her bonnet and leaned her head back with her face to the sun. "It is a beautiful day, isn't it?"

"It is that."

"The sky is so blue. And the only cloud is that big fluffy one over the mountains. Does that look like a storm cloud?"

"Yeah. But I think it's headed north." Travis examined the western sky.

The silence was broken by the jingle of the harness and the blowing of the horses. Travis glanced at Carrie. She had propped her feet on the front of the wagon and her elbows on the back of the seat. She was stretched out in the sun like a cat taking an afternoon nap. The sun glinted off of her hair and her skin was... Travis cleared his throat and concentrated on the road. Heat spread over his face and down his neck. When did the sun get so hot?

"Look!" Carrie sat up and pointed. "There's a doe and her fawn over there."

"I'll bet the buck is in that stand of trees. Maybe I should get out my rifle and go hunting."

Carrie slapped his arm. "Don't you dare! You leave that family alone."

Sparks flared on his skin from her touch. His arm felt like

it was on fire. How much farther? Too far.

"Why are we stopping?"

"We need to rest the horses, and this little brook is the perfect spot. You might as well get down and stretch your legs."

"I suppose so." Carrie climbed down unassisted. "It does feel good to stand up. The wind is beginning to blow."

"Mm-hmm. I noticed that storm cloud has changed direction. It may be coming our way." Travis surveyed the darkening sky.

"Do you think we'll get caught in the rain?"

"I don't know. All we can do is keep moving."

The clouds closed in fast. The wind gusted and whipped everything in its path. Travis squinted to keep the dust out of his eyes.

Carrie tightened her bonnet under her chin and tugged on the brim to cover her eyes.

"Here. Put this over your face." Travis handed Carrie his bandana. "It'll keep some of the dust out."

She covered her face with the unfolded cloth. It wasn't much, but it would help, anyway. Travis shoved his hat down on his head against the wind.

Plop! Plop! Plop! Big drops fell, one at a time. Big drops that felt like rocks falling out of the sky.

"Ow!" Carrie rubbed her arms and reached for a blanket.

Thunder rumbled across the valley like a drumroll. Lightening ripped open the sky and released a torrent of rain. Carrie's blanket did nothing to keep them dry.

"We need to find somewhere to get out of this rain," Travis yelled, to be heard over the storm. "Do you know of any shelter close by?"

"There's an old way station just up the road. It's been abandoned for a while, but it should still be standing," Carrie yelled back.

Travis nodded and jammed his hat harder on his head. *Please, Lord, I pray it's not too far.*

Carrie touched his arm and pointed through the rain. "There it is."

Travis squinted. Through the downpour, he could just make it out. "Thank you, Lord."

It wasn't much. At least it would be dry. And it had a stable for the horses. He lifted Carrie down from the wagon.

"I'm so cold." Carrie's teeth chattered and she shivered.

He lifted supplies out of the wagon. "We're both soaked to the skin. Let's get inside."

Chapter
Twenty-Three

The way station was one room with a large fireplace opposite the door, and a bed built into the wall to the right of the fireplace. A roughhewn table with four chairs sat in the middle of the room next to a large bear skin rug. A stove and shelves lined the wall opposite the bed. Nothing fancy. But it was sturdy and safe. And dry.

"Well, at least the roof doesn't leak." Travis set the supplies and his pack on the table. "We better get a fire going." He rubbed his hands together to get the blood circulating. "We'll have a nice fire in no time."

"This feels so much better." Carrie stretched her hands toward the growing flames.

"It'll take a few minutes to get the chill out of the room. But then it will be nice and warm. I'll get the rest of the supplies and take care of the horses." He dug a slicker out of his pack and slipped it on. "No sense in getting any wetter." He grinned and opened the door to brave the weather.

Carrie stayed in front of the fire. When would she stop shivering? Her hands were so cold, too. She sniffed as water dripped from her hair. How long would Travis be gone? Out in the storm? He'd need something to eat when he came back.

She looked through the supplies for anything that would pass as a meal. Why didn't she pack more food? They were supposed to be at Grace and Phillip's by supper. But she knew better. Peter had always said you should prepare for the worst and hope for the best.

She sighed. Well, that wouldn't help now. Their dinner would consist of bread, hard boiled eggs, and two apples. Carrie put her hands on her hips and chewed the inside of lip. Well, at least they wouldn't starve.

The door opened, and the storm drove Travis inside. "Hoowee! It's wet out there! Good thing I covered the wagon with a tarp." Water poured from his hat and dripped from his slicker. "I'm glad you knew about this place. I don't think we would have made it another mile. The road is getting pretty muddy."

"Do you think we'll be here long?"

"I don't know. If the rain stops soon, we might be able to go on. But, if it doesn't..." He shrugged out of his wet slicker.

"We could be here a while." He hung his hat and slicker on pegs by the door.

"Well, are you hungry? We have a few things that I packed for the trip. It won't keep us for long, but it will help." She spread her hands over their feast.

"No problem." Travis opened his pack on the table. He held up a tin can for Carrie to see. "That's why I always carry a can of beans. You never know when you're going to need it."

She cocked her head and lifted one eyebrow. Oh, fine. Did all men plan ahead? Carrie shivered again. She just could not get warm.

"We should get you out of those wet clothes."

"What?"

"Oh, I… uh… mean… you should hang your clothes up to dry… before you catch cold, I mean." He blushed as he reached for a blanket, which he hung over the rafter near the bed. "Here you go. You can change behind here and then put this other blanket on." He handed her another blanket. "Then you can hang your dress by the fire."

Carrie slipped behind the blanket and unbuttoned her dress. She shivered as it sagged to the floor before she peeled off her wet stockings. She wrapped the other blanket around her damp undergarments and emerged from the makeshift changing room.

"You can hang your clothes here by the fire." Travis pointed to nails on the mantle.

"Thank you." She hung laundry all the time. But hanging laundry while clinging to her dignity? That was new.

"Feel better?"

She turned to face Travis. "Yes, actually, I do. I've stopped shivering. Well, the dressing room is all yours." She pointed to the blanket he had hung for her.

"Oh, I'm all right. A little rain never hurt me. I've been wet before. "

"Aren't you cold?"

"A little. But I'll warm up soon enough. I'll put the beans in the fire to heat. When they're hot, we can eat." Travis opened the can and placed it at the edge of the flames.

"I'll slice the bread." Such a simple task proved more challenging than hanging her clothes. Thank goodness her back was to Travis. If he saw the blanket slip, he'd think she was shameless.

"I've never had beans cooked in a fire before." Carrie took

a bite of her bread.

"They're really good cooked over a camp fire. It gives them that special flavor." Travis spooned his last bite into his mouth.

He wouldn't look at her. Was she that unattractive? No. He was probably that uncomfortable. She was too.

He stood up without warning. "Let's see if the fire has done its job."

"Is it dry?" If only it was dry.

"The hem of your dress is."

"I hope they dry soon."

Another rumble of thunder rolled through the valley.

"I think this storm has set in for a while. I don't think we'll be going to your sister's tonight. We'll have to try first thing in the morning." Travis studied the fire.

"We're going to stay here? All night?" Carrie's voice rose in near panic. "But…"

"I don't see as we have any choice. The storm is too bad. We can't risk the horses or…"

"Where will we sleep? I mean, there's only one bed." Carrie's eyes grew wider. What was he suggesting? So, he did think she was shameless.

"Well… you can have the bed, and I'll sleep here in front

of the fire. We'll leave the blanket up for privacy." He glanced in her direction.

She looked at the bed. She looked at the rug. There couldn't have been more than five feet between them. Not a respectable distance. She gulped. What choice did they have? None.

"I suppose you're right. But I don't mind sleeping on the floor if you'd rather have the bed."

"Oh, no. I couldn't allow a lady to sleep on the floor while I slept in a comfortable bed. If my pa was here, he'd skin me alive. I'll be fine. Besides, I'm used to sleeping on the ground, and I've slept on harder places than this floor, believe me. This big bear rug will make a dandy bed. It's been a long time since I slept on a soft, warm bear rug." He looked around the cabin. "Well, it's getting dark, so I guess we better turn in. It could be a long day tomorrow."

"I suppose so." Carrie padded toward her makeshift bedroom. "Well, good night."

"Good night. Sleep well."

Carrie ducked behind the blanket that served as her bedroom door.

Chapter Twenty-Four

Travis had spent many nights by a fire. He was glad he wasn't out in the storm trying to stay dry that night. *Thank You, Lord, for once again providing for us with food and shelter. You never fail me. And Lord, thank You for the rain, even though it came a little too fast. But the farmers need it. And it will water our... I mean... Carrie's crops, too. Amen.*

He clasped his hands behind his head and stared at the ceiling. The crackle of the fire and the patter of the rain on the roof, they sounded like home. Home. That was such a long time ago. Too long.

He woke with a start and turned his head. "Carrie? What's wrong? Are you all right?"

She didn't answer. She just stood there, silhouetted against the fire. He propped himself up on one elbow and rubbed his eyes. She was still there.

She knelt, lifted the corner of his blanket, and slid underneath. Then, she put her hand on his shoulder and leaned in to kiss him. His breath caught in his throat and his senses whirled as her lips brushed his.

He pushed her away. "Carrie, what are you doing?"

"What does it look like I'm doing?" she whispered, and kissed him again.

"Carrie. No, this isn't right!" he whispered, his voice thick with emotion.

A mischievous grin lifted the corners of her mouth. "Well, maybe this will be better." She began kissing his neck.

"Carrie, stop! This is wrong."

She looked at him with fire in her eyes. "How can it be wrong to love me?"

She filled his senses. She filled his arms. He clawed at the fragments of his resolve. How could it be wrong?

A rumble of thunder vibrated the floor beneath them, and a flash of lightening shattered the darkness. They gasped and cowered together. The scene lit up like mid-day.

Darkness once again. He turned back to the woman in his arms. She was gone. He peered through the fire's glow. "Carrie? Where are you?"

Another streak of lightening. Again, the entire cabin was illuminated. There she was. Back in her bed. Was she hiding from the storm, or him?

"Carrie?" No answer. He crept toward the bed. She lay on her side, eyes closed, with her hands tucked under the pillow. The firelight danced across her face and hair.

"Carrie?" Did he dare touch her?

She rolled onto her back but didn't open her eyes. She just lay there in the firelight. Why didn't she open her eyes? She sighed. He noticed that the bodice of her chemise didn't quite conceal her full figure.

She wasn't asleep. Was she? But how could she have fallen asleep so fast? He held his breath. What if she'd always been asleep? What if she'd never been awake at all?

A blast of arctic air shot through him like a bolt of lightning. A dream. It was a dream! She hadn't come to him at all. Their moment together in front of the fire hadn't happened. He'd imagined it! He jumped back as if he'd been snake-bit, colliding with the table. His heart pounded in his ears like horse's hooves. He reeled toward the door, threw it open, and stumbled outside.

He hunched over, gasping for air. He lifted his head and welcomed the rain full in the face. *Oh Lord, thank You for the rain. Please help me. Please, God, quiet the storm that is brewing in my soul. And Lord, God, quench the fire that Carrie Lindquist is threatening to kindle within me. Give me the strength to do what You have called me to do.*

Chapter Twenty-Five

Carrie listened to the quiet. The rain had stopped. She opened her eyes and squinted against the sun shining through the window. She swung her legs over the side of the bed and sat up. The cold floor prickled her bare feet as she scurried to retrieve her clothes. They were dry. Ooh, and they were still warm.

The door opened and Travis entered the cabin.

"Good morning." Carrie peeked around the blanket curtain.

Travis dropped a load of wood in the firebox.

"Are you going to build another fire?"

"No. Refilling the box for the next visitor."

"Oh."

"I'm glad you're awake. We need to get going. I already loaded the supplies."

"Is the road very muddy? Will we be able to get through?"

"It's drying out. We may have to go slow, but we'll make it." He swung his pack from the table to his shoulder. "I'm going to hitch up the team while you get dressed."

"Travis?" She stopped him at the door. "Is something wrong?"

"No." He cleared his throat and spoke over his shoulder. "We should get on the road. Your family will be wondering what happened to you." The door shut behind him.

Carrie stared at the closed door. He sure was in a hurry to leave. He must have missed the children as much she did.

Carrie closed the door behind her and stepped into the sun. She inhaled the rain-washed air and viewed the countryside. Water droplets on the grass sparkled like diamonds. What a glorious morning. She climbed into the wagon and settled in the seat.

Travis finished hitching the team and climbed into the wagon in silence. He collected the reins and clucked to the team. The last few miles would be longer than all the others. She missed those babies so much.

Carrie studied Travis out of the corner of her eye. He stared at the road. Not a word. What happened? Did she say something wrong? Do something wrong?

Spending the night in the way station had been… awkward. But it was all very innocent. They had done nothing inappropriate. So, what was bothering him?

"Travis?"

"Hm." His eyes were fixed on the road.

"Are you sure there isn't anything wrong? Did I do something or say something…"

"No. Everything's fine."

"Are you sure?"

He seemed irritated by her questions. "I guess I didn't sleep very well last night."

"Maybe you should have taken the bed. I would have been glad to move to the bear rug." Did he just wince?

"Everything's fine."

He scowled and clenched his jaw. Everything was not fine. But he didn't want to discuss it. Carrie scanned the scenery. The sparkling diamond drops on the grass were gone. She sighed and tied her bonnet under her chin.

"How much farther is it?" Travis wondered.

"It should be just around the next big bend. The house will be off to the right. I wonder if the children have missed me."

"Not as much as you've missed them."

Chapter Twenty-Six

"Ma! Ma!" Nathan waved. "Abby, Emmy, Ma's here!" The siblings ran to meet the wagon as it pulled into the yard.

"Mama!" the girls cried together.

Carrie jumped down before Travis set the brake. "Oh, hello! How are you?" She gathered all three in a hug. "Did you have fun? Did you behave?"

"Hi, Aunt Carrie," Ruth and Levi shouted, running from the barn with Sarah in tow.

"Well, hello." Grace emerged from the house, wiping her hands on her apron. "We expected you yesterday. What happened?"

"We got caught in a rain storm and had to wait it out." Carrie lifted Emily into her arms.

"Oh, we saw that storm to the east. Phillip wondered if you might have gotten caught in it."

"You could say that."

"I miss you, Mama." Emily wrapped her little arms around her mother's neck.

"I missed you, too." Carrie squeezed her tight.

"Hello, Travis. How are you?" Grace greeted him.

"Fine," he answered, as Abigail ran to him. He picked her up and whirled her around before setting her back on her feet.

"Travis, guess what?" Nathan pulled on Travis' arm.

"What?"

"Uncle Phillip took us fishin' and I caught one this big!" He held his hands out the measured length.

"You don't say. Well, good for you." He tousled the boy's blond mop.

"I don't like fishin'. Oooh, worms," Abigail shuddered.

"Girls," Nathan complained, as Travis laughed.

"Well, come in. I have some cold cider waiting for you." Grace waved them toward the house.

"Oh, that will taste good." Carrie followed her sister inside.

"All right, children. Run along now. You don't have much time left to play together, so you best make the most of it." Grace shooed the children outside. "So, what happened with the rain? Did you really get caught in it?"

"Yes, we did. Fortunately, we were almost to that old way station when it started. It was like the sky just opened up. We had to spend the night in that old place." Carrie took the glass

Grace offered her.

"Really? It's a wonder that old place is still standing. There hasn't been a stage through there in almost three years."

"It almost looked like someone was still living there. Didn't it, Travis?"

"Hm? Oh, yeah, it was good and sound. Even the stable. It was a good thing. That storm was bad."

"Well, I'm glad you were safe. Nate and Abby were worried because you didn't come last night." Grace took a chair at the table.

"Oh dear. Were they very upset?" Carrie sat across from her.

"Phillip was able to distract them all with a game. This morning they were much better."

"Oh, good. Where is Phillip?"

"He's dropping off a load of firewood at the Wyatt's. He'll be back before lunch. Which reminds me, I better get it started. Do you want more cider, Travis?"

"Just a little, thanks. That's mighty good cider. Do you make it yourself?"

"Thank you. Phillip makes it every fall. Carrie and the kids come, and we make it a family project. Simon will be big enough to help this year."

"I thought it tasted familiar." He emptied his glass. "Well, I best see to the horses."

"What can I do to help with lunch?" Carrie pushed herself out of the chair.

"Well… you can slice the potatoes while I do the carrots." Grace handed her a knife. "It's too bad we don't have any of the mutton left from supper last night. I swear those children were ravenous. They ate every bit of it." Grace shook her head.

"I'm not surprised. It takes a lot of food to feed seven children and a hungry husband." Carrie grabbed a potato and began slicing. "Grace, I need to talk to you about something."

"What's on your mind?"

"I had a talk with Nathan recently. He knows what really happened to Peter."

Grace froze in mid-motion and looked up at her sister. "How could he? He wasn't old enough to know anything."

Carrie studied Grace's face. "Well… he said that he overheard you and Phillip talking about it."

"What?" Grace dropped her knife. "When? I swear we never said anything… I don't know when he could have heard us. I mean, we haven't even talked about Peter for a long time."

"He didn't say when it was."

"Oh, Carrie. I am so sorry. We know how you feel about the children knowing what really happened. We would never tell them. I… don't know what to say."

"Oh, I know you didn't mean for him to hear. And I'm not trying to accuse you… I just wanted you to know."

"Did he say anything else? How did it make him feel about his pa?"

"He wanted to know if Peter was a bad man. I told him that his pa thought he was doing the right thing, even though I still don't understand how he could have believed that."

"Good. It's important for a boy to be able to look up to his father. Why didn't he tell you before?"

"He thought I really believed that Peter had died in an accident. He was trying to protect me." Tears pooled in Carrie's eyes. "I can't believe he kept it a secret. All this time. I feel so sorry for him, and yet I'm so proud of him."

Grace wrapped both arms around Carrie. "You should be proud. He's quite a boy."

Phillip burst through the door. "Hey you two, how long until lunch? You've got some hungry men and children out here."

Grace jumped and released Carrie. "Oh, you're back. Lunch

will be ready in about thirty minutes."

"Good. I'll put my tools away and wash up." He turned to go back outside.

"Make sure the children are washed too, please."

"Yes, ma'am," he teased, closing the door behind him.

Chapter Twenty-Seven

"I swear, you two girls… If you pull those clothes off of the line and get them dirty, I'll shine your backsides."

With the entire yard to roam in, why did Abigail and Emily insist on playing tag in the clean laundry?

"Abigail! That's enough! You two go play somewhere else. You've all been as wild as a pack of wolves since you got back. What's gotten into you?"

All three of them were out of sorts. Emily was the worst. Sluggish and moody, not eating much. She was just too young to be away from home for so long.

"I could sure use some sweet little hands to help me over here," Travis announced from across the yard. "Nathan and I have almost finished the weathervane. Do you want to help put it up?"

"I wanna help," Abigail squealed, and dashed off.

"Emily, don't you want to help Travis and Nathan?" Carrie picked up a shirt to hang in the sun.

"No."

"Why not?" The little girl shrugged. "Well, you don't have to actually do anything. You can just watch. Go see what they're doing." Carrie nudged her shoulder. "Go on."

Emily trudged away. No spunk. No energy. Well, a few more days of rest and routine and she'd be more herself. A mother could always hope.

Carrie turned back to the basket of wet clothes. She held a dress by the sleeve and secured it on the line. Travis had been out of sorts, too, since the children had come home. No, that wasn't true. He was different the morning after the storm. But why?

That was the worst storm she'd seen in years, and they were lucky that way station was still there. They had no choice but to stay the night. Her cheeks warmed at the memory of trying to keep her blanket closed. It had been more than a little awkward. But nothing happened. So that couldn't be what troubled Travis. But something did.

"Hooray! Ma, it's done," Nathan hollered across the yard.

Travis held up the finished weathervane. "How does it look?"

"It's great!" Nathan's grin covered his face.

Carrie left the empty basket and joined the celebration.

"Yeah! We made a good wetter vane," Abigail stated with pride.

"You? We made it. Travis and me. All you did was paint the rooster's tail," Nathan pointed out.

"I still helped," Abigail defended herself.

"You all helped. I couldn't have done it without any of you," Travis smiled at Abigail.

"Where are we gonna put it?" Nathan scanned the roof of the house.

"What about right over the door? Then you'll know which way to spit before you leave the house." Travis elbowed Nathan, and they laughed at his joke.

Carrie frowned and cocked one eyebrow. Oh, fine. Travis hadn't lost his bad sense of humor.

"Do you like it?" Nathan looked at his ma for approval.

"Yes. It's perfect." It would look nice on top of the roof. "You all better get cleaned up for supper soon."

"Hear that? If we don't get this mess cleaned up, we might go hungry 'til morning." Travis led the way to the barn.

Emily lagged behind. "Mama…"

"Yeah?" Carrie answered over her shoulder, on her way

back to her own task.

"Mama?"

Carrie turned to face her youngest. "What's wrong?"

"I don't feel good."

"Does your stomach hurt?" Emily shook her head. "Does your head hurt?" She nodded. Carrie pressed her hand to the child's forehead. "Go on in the house. I'll get my basket and be right there."

Emily struggled to take a few steps. Poor baby. Carrie tucked a loose hair behind her ear and started toward the empty basket, waiting to be filled yet again. Without warning, Emily collapsed like an empty flour sack before she even reached the porch.

"Emily!" Carrie ran and dropped in the dirt, scooping her baby into her arms. "Emily! Emmy!" No response.

Her little body was so limp. "No! No!" Help. She needed help. "Travis! Travis!"

She cuddled Emily and whispered in her ear. "It's all right, Emmy. Mama's here. It's going to be all right." Her tears washed the dust from the girl's face.

"What happened?" Travis' voice reached her ear. His face appeared out of nowhere.

"I don't know. She said… she didn't feel good." Tears all but choked out her words. "And I … we were going into the… house. And she collapsed. And I can't wake her up. Oh, Travis!" She buried her face in Emily's hair.

"Get her bed." Travis lifted Emily like she was made of glass. She looked so small in his big arms.

Carrie pushed herself to her feet. She hurried to the house on wobbly legs that threatened to give way. She made it to Emily's bed and ripped back the covers.

Travis laid the girl down and felt her head. "Did she say anything? Did she complain of anything?" He felt her stomach.

"She said her head hurt." Carrie bit the inside of her lip and wiped the tears from her face.

"Let's get her undressed." Travis removed Emily's shoes.

Carrie unbuttoned the little girl's dress. "Do you know what's wrong with her?"

Travis let out a heavy sigh. "You better get the doctor."

"We don't have a doctor!"

"You don't have a doctor?"

"No. I told you that before, remember? What are we going to do?"

A shadow swept across Travis' face. His jaw clenched and

unclenched.

"What is it? It's bad, isn't it?" She sighed and looked at Emily. "Oh, Travis…"

"I'm a doctor."

"What?"

"I am a doctor—or, I was a doctor." He looked at Carrie through the shadow covering his face.

"What? Wait… what do you mean?"

"I'll explain later. I promise. But right now, we need to take care of Emily."

Chapter

Twenty-Eight

Travis stood frozen. He'd made a vow, to God and to himself. A vow he swore he'd never break. But Emily needed his help. Carrie needed his help. *God, You know my heart. Please show me what to do.*

"We need to get her fever down. Get water and cloths. Do you have any willow bark?"

Carrie nodded. "It's what I gave you for your fever."

"Good; brew some tea."

"What's wrong with her?"

Travis rolled up his sleeves. "I don't know, but we should probably move Abby out of here." He sat on the bed and took Emily's hand. It was burning up. "Hurry with the water and tea."

Emily coughed, hard. He'd heard that cough before. Too many times. Please, don't let it be that. *Oh, Lord, please help me. Please help Emily.*

"Mama?" Emily moaned.

"Yes, sweetheart?"

"My head hurts."

"Do you hurt anywhere else?"

"My throat hurts, too."

Carrie caressed Emily's little hand. It was so hot. "Shh. Just rest, baby. Go back to sleep."

"Hey," Travis whispered from the doorway, with another cup of coffee. Carrie looked up at him, bleary-eyed. "You need to get some sleep. There's no sense in both of us being up all night."

"You're the one who needs sleep." How could she leave Emily's side?

"I'll nap on Abigail's bed if I need to. Now, go on." Travis set his coffee cup on the table by the bed.

"I'm all right."

"No, you're not. I'll call you if I need you. Doctor's orders." He grimaced at his own words.

"All right. But you call me, even if you don't need me." Carrie pushed herself out of the chair. "I'm going to check on

Nathan and Abigail first."

"Fine."

Carrie eased Nathan's bedroom door open and tiptoed over to the bed. He and Abigail were sound asleep in Nathan's bed. The moonlight streaming through the window illuminated their faces. They looked like angels.

"Good night, my loves." She leaned over to kiss them both. Abigail's head felt like a branding iron. Fever!

"Mama, my head hurts real bad," the girl muttered.

Carrie tore from Nathan's room and swung around the door frame where Emily slept.

"Abby! She's sick too!" She gasped. "She's burning up with fever, and her head hurts!"

Travis bolted from his seat and into Nathan's room. Without a word, he scooped Abigail from Nathan's bed and carried her out the door.

"What's going on?" Nathan sat up, rubbing his eyes.

"We're just moving Abby back to her bed."

"Why?"

"It's all right. Just go back to sleep." Carrie bent to kiss him. No fever. A sigh of relief escaped her lips.

"The sun will be up soon." Carrie sighed and looked out the window. She stretched her back and turned back to the room.

"It's been a long night." Travis wiped his face with his hands.

"Their fevers aren't coming down, and their coughs are getting worse by the minute. Do you have any idea what it is?" She fought back tears and chewed the inside of her lip.

"I've seen something like it before. But this isn't nearly as bad."

"Seen what? What is it?" She looked at her daughters, lying helpless in their beds. "Don't you know?" Her eyes filled with tears.

Travis ushered her out of the tiny bedroom and closed the door behind them. "I don't know for sure. The fever and cough are troubling."

"Troubling, how? You've seen this before? Where?"

"I've seen something like it. But it was worse, much worse." And spread like prairie fire through the camps.

"What was it?"

"Camp fever."

Carrie's eyes grew to the size of silver dollars. "Where would they have gotten that?"

"They didn't. I said it was similar. That's not what Abigail and Emily have." At least, he prayed not.

"Well, whatever they have, what can we do about it?"

"Does Jack Dawson have quinine?"

"I don't know."

"I'll find out. But for now, we need mustard plasters and more willow bark tea."

"How did they come down with this?"

"Has anyone you know been sick?"

Carrie shook her head.

"What about the Baxters? Maybe one of them was sick, and they didn't know it yet when the girls were there."

She gasped in horror. "Nathan! Will he get sick, too? And Grace and Phillip and the children. Are they all going to get sick? What if... are they going to die? What if they..."

"Carrie." Travis grabbed her by both arms. "Carrie, stop!"

"My babies. I can't lose my babies." Tears coursed down her cheeks.

"Carrie!" He pulled her into his arms to quiet her for a moment, before he pushed her back until his face was inches from hers. His voice was low and intense. "If you want to fall apart, fine. But you do it outside. You are not going to do it in here where those girls can hear you. They're sick and scared. They need to believe that they're going to be all right. They need you to believe it, too." She just stared at him. He tightened his grip on her arms and pulled her closer until their noses touched. "Understand?"

She closed her eyes and gave a nod. "But what do we do?"

"I'm doing everything I know how to do. Now, we just need to pray and trust God to do His part. You need to pray, too."

She stepped back and he let go of her arms. Her hands flew to her face and she ran to the door, flung it open, and stumbled outside.

Carrie wandered out into the morning sun. Travis was right. She had to pull herself together. But her babies. And Nathan. What if he got sick, too? What would she do…? And Grace and her family? They had to be all right. They just had to be. She could pray, but why?

"It probably won't do any good. But…" She leaned her head on the top rail of the corral fence, eyes closed.

After everything that had happened, now this? She could lose the one thing she had left. Would God take her children, too?

"Dear God. I don't know if You're listening, but Travis says You do. He said that You love me and my children. Abigail and Emily are so sick. Travis says they have some kind of fever. He's doing all he can. He says we need to ask You to do your part. Oh God, please help them. My children are all I have. Please God, please, don't take them away from me. I can't bear to lose them."

Her tears soaked her dress sleeve. Tears of desperation, sadness, relief. Was that what it felt like to pour your heart out to God?

Chapter Twenty-Nine

"Good morning."

Travis greeted Nathan as he entered the kitchen, rubbing his eyes. "How are you feeling?" He studied the boy for any signs of sickness.

"I'm okay. Just tired. How come you came and got Abby last night?" He yawned and stretched.

"She is sick, too, so we put her back in her own bed."

"What's wrong with her and Emily?"

The kitchen door opened, and Carrie returned from outside. "Good morning, Nathan. Are you feeling all right?"

"How come everybody keeps asking me how I feel? I'm fine." He squirmed in is chair. "So, what's wrong with Abby and Emmy?"

"They have a fever and cough." Travis scooped eggs onto plates. "Was anyone sick at your cousins' house?"

"No. Nobody but Buster.

"Buster? The dog?"

"Yeah. The first night we were there, Abigail and Emily kept trying to get him to eat. And then the next day he was throwing up all over the place. I think they made him sicker. Uncle Phillip told them to leave him alone. He wouldn't let any of us go near Buster after that."

"What happened to Buster? Did he get better?"

"I don't know. He was still sick when we left."

"Could they have gotten something from the dog?" Carrie eyed Travis.

"Could be. If so, I wouldn't know what it is." Travis rubbed his neck. "Well, sit down and eat some breakfast, and I'll check on the girls." He set two plates on the table.

"I'm not hungry." Carrie poured a cup of coffee.

"You need to eat anyway." He tapped the plate in her direction. "I'll be right back."

"You need to go rest." Travis pulled Carrie out of the rocking chair beside Abigail's bed.

"You haven't left this room for more than a few minutes for two days."

"No. I'm fine. But I do need to get some more water."

Travis took the pitcher from her hands. "Nathan can get

the water. You need to rest."

"But…"

"I'll make sure he keeps his distance. Don't worry."

"I'm not tired, really." She had no time to be tired. Her babies needed her.

Travis eyed her as if she were one of her girls, caught in a fib. "Don't lie to the doctor. He knows better." He ushered her to the door. "Go. Lie down for a while."

"But what if they need me?" What if Abigail or Emily called for her and she wasn't there?

"I'll wake you. I promise. You're just a few steps away."

Carrie sighed and wiped her forehead with the back of her hand. "All right. But just for a little while."

A few steps away? At that moment her room seemed a mile away. She closed the door behind her and sat on the bed. Her eyes burned like hot embers, and every muscle ached. She closed her burning eyes and rubbed her temples. Her head pounded like a cattle stampede.

How could life change so fast from one day to the next, without warning? Like when Peter died. Life changed forever in a matter of moments, without her knowledge or consent.

"Travis!"

Travis looked up from Emily's bed. "Nate, what's wrong?"

"It's Ma. She looks funny."

Travis raced ahead of Nathan to Carrie's room. She lay crumpled in a heap on the bed. His mouth went dry as edged toward her. No, not Carrie too. Her forehead was cool. No fever. *Thank You, Lord.* He further examined her for familiar symptoms.

"Mama… is she… is she sick?" Nathan's young face was etched with fear.

Travis shook his head and looked up at the boy still standing in the doorway. "No. She's going to be fine. She's just worn out."

Relief flooded through Travis like a tide as he covered her with a blanket. He closed the bedroom door behind them.

"Let's just leave her alone and let her get some rest."

Chapter Thirty

"My head doesn't hurt anymore," Emily smiled up at Travis.

"Good. That's very good." He felt her head and listened to her chest.

"Can I go play now?" The little girl's eyes pleaded with him.

"Oh, no. I'm afraid not."

"I feel better, too. Why can't we go play?" Abigail whined from her bed.

"You may be feeling better, but you're a long way from being well. You're both going to have to stay in bed for a few more days."

"Oh," they complained in unison.

"Now, girls. You heard what Travis said." Carrie straightened Abigail's covers. "Are you hungry?"

"Do we have to have broth again?" Abigail continued to whine.

"Well, I think we could try something else tonight. How does that sound?" The girls nodded. "How about some bread and jam?"

"Yeah!" Emily clapped her hands.

"A big piece of bread, with lots of jam." Abigail motioned to her mother.

"I'll see what I can do."

"Not too big, and not too much jam," Travis cautioned Carrie as she left the room. "Now, you two eat your bread and promise me you'll stay in bed. We'll see what tomorrow brings."

The girls nodded.

Travis made his way out to the kitchen table and sank into a chair. "They're making good progress. In a few more days, they'll be able to be up and around."

"You need rest." Carrie set a cup of coffee on the table in front of him. "You can go get some sleep. I'll look after Abby and Emmy."

He reached for the cup, took a sip, and nodded. "Fine. Just give them each one slice of bread for now. They need to take it slow." He put his hands on the table and pushed himself out of the chair.

"Can I have some bread and jam too, Ma?" Nathan licked his lips.

"Yes, but then you need to get straight to bed. It's getting late." Carrie cut another slice.

"Nate, come and get me if your Ma needs me."

The boy nodded his head and spread jam on a thick slab of bread.

Travis lit the lamp and slumped on the edge of his bed. He rubbed his face and shook his head. He'd seen fevers before. So many men had died from mysterious fevers during the war. And he had been helpless to stop it. Those two little girls were a miracle, plain and simple.

Oh, Lord, I can't thank You enough for what You've done. Thank You for working in the lives of Abigail and Emily and for restoring them to health. Thank You for giving them back to their mother. I don't think Carrie could have stood losing them. Please, forgive me for breaking my vow. But thank You for using me here in this place. What a tremendous display of Your power and love. Thank You, Lord. Amen.

When was the last time he'd been so tired? It was a long time ago. During the war. And when Elizabeth died. In all the years since, he'd never felt so spent. He groaned as he swung his legs up on the bed. He closed his eyes and sank into the mattress.

There was a tap at the door, and he opened his eyes. Nathan? Carrie needed him? Abigail or Emily was in trouble—or both?

He struggled to sit up.

"Come in." He pushed himself to his feet as Carrie entered his room. "What's happened? Are the girls all right?"

"They're fine. They ate their bread and went to sleep."

"Phew. You had me worried." Carrie didn't move. "Is there something else?"

"Yes. I… just wanted… to thank you for what you've done." Her voice was thick with emotion and tears. She crossed the space between them. "I can't believe we escaped another tragedy. I don't know what we would have done without you. How can I ever thank you?" She wrapped her arms around Travis' neck.

He closed his arms around her, holding her close. He could feel her breath on his face as their eyes met. The scent of her filled his nostrils. The now-familiar aroma of her. Before he could react, her lips were on his. He battled again not to respond to her kiss. But this time, the battle was real.

"Wait. Carrie." He pulled her arms from his neck.

She yanked her arms back and her hands flew to her mouth. She turned away from him. "I am so sorry."

Travis grabbed her arm before she could escape. "No," he groaned. "No, Carrie, don't be sorry. I… I just don't want you to confuse gratitude with… with something else."

She pulled her arm from his grasp and turned back to face him. "I… just wanted to thank you for saving my children."

"I didn't save your children, Carrie. God did. He may have used me, but He performed the miracle."

Without a word she whirled and ran out of the room, leaving the door standing open behind her.

Chapter Thirty-One

Abigail and Emily didn't move. Travis felt their heads and listened to their breathing. No sign of the fever returning, and they were resting well. *Thank You again, Lord, for what You have done. Only You could have performed this miracle, and I am truly grateful.*

"Good morning," Travis greeted Carrie, as he entered the kitchen from the girls' room.

Carrie turned from the stove with the spoon in her hand. "Breakfast will be ready soon. Would you like some coffee?"

"Please. Abby and Emmy are doing fine this morning."

"They slept the night through. For the first time since they got sick."

"That's good news. They should be able to get out of bed for a short time today."

Nathan poured milk into a glass and helped his mother dish up the eggs and biscuits.

"Hi, Travis." He was his usual cheerful self. "Ma said that

Abigail and Emily are going to be okay. That you saved them."

"Well, I just helped. The Lord did the hard work."

"Well, we are still very grateful for all you've done." Carrie sat down at the table. "I've been thinking that it would be so good to have a doctor around here again. Cedar Creek really needs a doctor." She looked up at him.

What was she saying? Did she think he would stay? Did she want him to stay? Oh, no. He had to leave. Now, more than ever.

"Are you going to stay, Travis?" Nathan set his milk glass down with a thump. "Gee, that would be great! We could practice and really whip everybody at the picnic next year." He shoved a bite of biscuit into his mouth and grinned.

"Whoa, now." Travis held up his hands. "I never said I would stay."

"Well, where would you go?" Nathan looked confused.

"Where I've been going for the last five years. Wherever God leads me."

"Did He lead you to us?"

"Yes, I believe He did, because you needed help. But now it's time for me to move on and help someone else."

"Nathan, finish your breakfast and go collect the eggs,"

Carrie interrupted him.

He swallowed the rest of his milk and headed for the door.

"Clear your dirty dishes first."

He hurried back and put his dishes in the sink and left the house.

Travis scooped up his eggs with his biscuit and took a bite. He chewed on his breakfast—and on what Carrie had said.

"You're leaving, then?" Carrie broke the silence. "Why?"

"As I said, it's time for me to move on." He stared into his coffee cup.

"When will you go?"

"I'm not sure. Soon, but I want to make sure the girls are back on their feet first." He took a sip from his cup and set it back on the table.

"Why didn't you tell me you were a doctor? Why did you keep that a secret?"

Because he wasn't a doctor. Not anymore.

"I don't understand why you don't stay here. In town, I mean. You know how much we need a doctor. You would have more patients than you know what to do with."

Travis sighed and fidgeted in his chair. "You don't understand. I just can't stay."

"Why not? Don't you like it here? Is it because of last night? I admit I behaved shamefully, and I am sorry. It'll never happen again. I promise. Please don't let my lapse in judgment drive you away."

He shook his head. "No, it has nothing to do with last night. I just can't stay."

"But why? Can't you at least tell me that? You promised you would."

Could he tell her? Should he tell her? He *had* promised he would explain. Why did he do that? He closed his eyes laid his head in his hands. *Lord, please give me the words. Give me the courage. Thank You, Lord.* He lifted his head and looked across the table at Carrie.

"During the war, I was a doctor in the Union Army in Virginia. My wife, Elizabeth, was at home in Pennsylvania when a patrol of Confederate soldiers came through." He was about to strangle on the knot in his throat. *Lord, give me strength. Please.*

"What happened?" Carrie coaxed him.

"The whole patrol was sick with the cholera. The doctor set up a hospital in the train station to care for all of the sick, and the wounded, too. Some of the women volunteered to help him, including Elizabeth. Despite all of their efforts, almost all the soldiers died—and most of the volunteers."

"Elizabeth?" Carrie spoke a little above a whisper.

Travis closed his eyes and nodded. "By the time I got the news, she had been gone for months."

"I'm so sorry."

"As soon as I was free of the army, I vowed I would never practice medicine again."

"But why?"

"If I'd been home where I belonged, I could have saved Elizabeth, maybe even some of the others. But I had to be noble and support the war effort. I thought I could do more good caring for the soldiers. Ha!" A lot of good that had done. Most of them died anyway.

"But maybe you wouldn't have been able to save Elizabeth, even if you had been home."

"Exactly. So, what good was it to be a doctor at all, when I couldn't save the one person in the world who was most precious to me?"

"Travis, you can't blame yourself."

He shook his head and shrugged. "I couldn't stay in Pennsylvania without Elizabeth, so I sold everything I owned and left. I've been travelling ever since."

"And you think God brought you here?"

He nodded.

"Listen, I appreciate all that you've done on the farm. You've helped us more than you know. But Abigail and Emily would have died if you hadn't been here. We need you. Cedar Creek needs you."

He jumped up, almost tipping his chair. "I can't stay! Don't you see?"

"No. I don't see. You claim you want to help people, but by turning your back on medicine you're refusing to do the one thing that could help them the most." Carrie looked him in the eye. "You said I was blaming God for what Peter did. But you're doing the same thing."

"How? I'm not blaming God."

"You're blaming the wrong person. You're blaming yourself for what happened. And you're trying to make up for it by not practicing medicine and travelling all over creation, supposedly helping people. No matter how many times you help some family in trouble, you'll never be free of your guilt. You can't run from yourself. Wherever you go, you'll always be there." She gripped the edge of the table. "Travis, I believe in you. But you need to believe in yourself."

"The fact is that I was a doctor, and I couldn't save my own wife. I loved her so much, and I failed her. I can't fail anyone else. I just can't do that again." He raked his fingers through his hair and paced to the window.

"So, you're afraid."

Afraid of what? Failure? Yes, he was.

"Travis, you have a gift. A gift of knowledge that few people have. If you don't use a gift you've been given, then it just goes to waste."

"You should talk about being afraid and going to waste! You're holed up here on this farm feeling sorry for yourself. Fear and shame are holding you prisoner. You're a wonderful person, Carrie, and you have a great deal to give people, but you're afraid to trust anyone. Afraid to let anyone near you or your children. Your neighbors want to help you, like the Dawsons, and Reverend Chandler, and the Shafers, even Liza Martin. But you continually shun them and push them away. You're just wasting the rest of your life away."

Travis slammed the kitchen door as he left the house and stomped off the porch. How dare she accuse him of being afraid? Fear clutched her so tight she couldn't even breathe.

He heard the thud of something hitting the wall and the clank of a tin coffee cup rolling on the floor. Then a door slammed. Sadness surrounded him like a shroud.

He knelt by the side of his bed dropped his head in his hands. *Oh, Lord. Please help Carrie to understand. I made a promise to You. I've already broken part of it, and I just can't go back on the rest. I don't want to hurt her. She's been hurt enough. But I really have to go. Please help her to understand. And help me to have the courage to leave. Amen.* He lifted his Bible from the trunk by his bed and opened it. Maybe reading his favorite passages would strengthen his resolve.

Travis settled his saddle bags on the flanks of his horse and began to tie them down. Where would God lead him next? He reached for his bedroll, but footsteps in the dirt stopped him. Carrie stood just inside the barn door. Her eyes were filled with sadness.

"What are the girls up to?" Thank goodness they were almost back to themselves.

"Oh, they're just enough better to be underfoot." Carrie gave him half a smile. "But I'm thankful they are still with me to be under my feet."

Travis smiled and nodded. He untied the reins of his horse and backed him out of the stall. "I said goodbye to the children already. I'm going to miss them."

"They're going to miss you, too. They've come to love you. It has been so good for them to have a man around again. They thought you were going to stay."

"I never said I would stay. I said from the beginning I was just passing through." He tightened the cinch on his saddle.

"I know. But it doesn't make it any easier." Carrie looked down at her folded hands and back up. She bit the inside of her lip. "I know you think you have to go…" She swallowed hard. "But… I wish you could stay." Her voice quivered.

Travis dropped the reins and strode to where she stood. He took her arms in both of his large hands and looked into her eyes. He pulled her close, pressed his lips to her forehead, and released her. "You take care of yourself, Carrie Lindquist," he whispered, his voice thick with emotion. Letting her go was harder than he'd imagined. Then he swung into the saddle and rode out of the barn without looking back.

Chapter Thirty-Two

"Can I have more stew?" Abigail handed her plate to Carrie.

"'May I have more stew, please?'" Carrie corrected her.

"May I have more stew, puhlease?"

"You're sure feeling better. You're back to your sassy self, Miss Abigail." Carrie refilled the plate and handed it back to the girl.

"Thank you," Abigail responded.

"That's better," Carrie nodded, and smiled. "Do you want more stew, Nathan?"

"Nah."

"'No, thank you'? Honest to goodness, what's happened to you all? One little sickness, and you forget everything you've been taught."

"No, thank you." Nathan took a bite of his biscuit.

"But stew is your favorite. And I made oatmeal pie for dessert."

"I'm not hungry."

"Turning down stew and oatmeal pie? Are you feeling all

right? You're not getting sick now, are you?"

"No, Ma. I'm just not hungry. May I be excused?"

Well, at least he remembered something. "Yes, put your dishes up."

"I want pie." Emily raised her hand.

"You finish your stew first, then we'll talk about it." Carrie took a bite from her own plate.

"Mama, can we have a story after supper?" Abigail wiped stew from her mouth.

"Don't we always? Nathan, why don't you pick out a story?"

Carrie settled into her chair and the children sat on the floor. There was a chill in the air. She pulled her shawl tighter around her shoulders.

"Here, Ma. Read this one." Nathan pointed out the story he had chosen.

"All right." She cleared her throat. "Once upon a time…"

"I wish Travis was here to read to us. He made the stories funny." Abigail pouted and leaned back on her arms.

"I liked his make-believe stories the best," Nathan added.

"I miss Tavis." Emily's chin quivered as she lowered it into her hands.

"Oh, dear, what am I going to do with all of you? Travis is gone, and there's nothing we can do about it." Three somber faces stared up at her. "I'll miss him, too. He was a good friend to this family. But all we can do now is thank God for sending him to us when we needed him, and pray that God will keep him safe." Did she just say that? Did she mean it?

"Can we pray now?" Nathan sat up on his knees.

"Well, I guess so." Carrie squirmed in her chair. She wasn't going to pray out loud, in front of her children. "Would one of you would like to do it?"

"I will!" Abigail raised her hand.

"Okay, go ahead. Let's all bow our heads and fold our hands." That's how it was done, wasn't it?

Abigail's small voice rang out strong and clear. "Dear God. Please take care of Travis and keep him safe. And tell him that we miss him. Amen."

"Where did you learn to pray like that?" She had never taught them anything like that, and neither had Peter.

"Travis taught us." Nathan revealed the truth.

Of course. Only Travis would think to teach little ones to pray. He really was something. "Well, I think you all better get into bed. It's getting late."

"But Ma, we didn't have a story," Nathan protested.

"No arguing, now. Do as you're told. I'll be in in a minute. Abigail, can you help Emily with her night clothes, please?"

"Yes, Mama."

"Thank you."

Travis taught her children to pray. He taught her to pray. She leaned her head back in the rocker and closed her eyes.

Lord, please watch over Travis. Thank You for sending him to help us. And, Lord, thank You for healing my children. Travis said You performed a miracle, and I believe him. And I believe in You. I believe that You do love me and my children. Forgive me, Lord. Please.

How could they all miss him so much, when he had been with them for such a short time? But he had done so much. He had repaired the barn and the fences and the house, and planted crops in the field, and set Carrie up in the egg business. He saved her farm. Their home. She was now indebted to him but could never repay him for all he had done.

He'd opened her heart to feel again. To feel peace, and joy, and love. And, he opened her eyes to the truth about Peter and about God. She never thanked him for that.

Travis had more influence on her little family in a few months than some men have in a lifetime. Perhaps even Peter.

Chapter Thirty-Three

Travis took a bite of beans. They used to taste so good cooked over a campfire. Maybe Carrie's cornbread would made them taste better. She made the best cornbread.

He had shared his last can of beans with Carrie. The two of them alone. That night in the way station. In the raging storm. It haunted him.

She had stood in front of the fire and then slipped into his bed. Where did that come from? He hadn't thought of Carrie in that way. Or had he? It was a crazy dream. He shook his head to erase the memories. He had to forget that night, put it behind him.

The flames of the campfire burned low. He finished his cup of coffee and stared into the fire until it was coals. He emptied the coffee pot over the embers and wrapped himself in his bedroll. Lying on his back, he studied the stars. They were so small, so far away in the huge black canopy. He was alone. More alone than he'd been in a very long time.

He closed his eyes and the children's laughter rang in his ears. Their faces appeared in front of him: Nathan, Abigail, and Emily. He rather favored Emily, with her curls and chubby little fingers and her mother's eyes. Then Carrie's face was before him. She smiled at him with that twinkle in her eye. He'd only seen that spark a few times, and it was a rare treat.

"Aaaah!" he grumped out loud, and flopped onto his side. He needed to get to sleep. By the next night he intended to have put a fair distance between himself and the Lindquist farm.

How could he sleep? His mind swirled like a prairie tornado. When Elizabeth died, he'd left everything. He began to roam, never staying long anywhere. He liked it that way. Or, he'd grown accustomed to it. But his memories always went with him. Now, again, his thoughts were filled with what he'd left behind. His heart was like lead in his chest.

Oh, Father God. Show me what to do. You know the vow I made to You, and I don't want to break it. If there are more people out there that need my help, then just keep me pressing on. I want to do what You want me to do...

Another image appeared before his eyes. It was the image of a man. A man alone. A man trying to outrun himself. In search of something. Something to fill the need inside him.

A need he'd denied for too long. It gnawed at him. It clawed at him.

He had longed to be a father, but Elizabeth couldn't bear children. He'd prayed for a miracle that had never happened. He sat up and crossed his legs and leaned on his elbows. He subdued his grief. Tamed it, like a monster in a cage, fighting to be free.

"Oh, Lord, You know the desire of my heart is to serve You," Travis spoke into the darkness. "Since you took Elizabeth home there's been such an ache in my soul. All this time, I've been asking why? Was this for the best? It's hard to believe that taking the love of my life was for my best... To leave me alone, with all this guilt." He sucked in a ragged breath.

"But Lord, I understand, now. Even if I'd been home, I couldn't have saved Elizabeth. I didn't fail her. Carrie was right. Father, Carrie was right! I know it was Your plan for her to go live with You. Oh, Lord, thank You for the truth, and for Your peace."

His horse whinnied and stomped the ground. Travis met the animal's gaze. "Oh, fine. Now you're on her side, too. Just eat your grass."

Travis adjusted his position on the ground. Too bad the fire was out. A cup of coffee would taste good about now.

"And, Lord, please, tell me what I should do about Carrie, and Nathan, and Abigail, and Emily. You know this yearning in my heart for a family. A family of my own. Those children are so precious to me. They've all moved into my heart, and I will never be able to get them out. If I am not to return to them, I'll need Your help, Lord, to let them and their mother go."

Five years he'd been running, but he couldn't outrun himself. Carrie was right about that, too. He'd packed his guilt in his saddlebags and had taken it with him everywhere he went. He'd stopped believing in himself. But Carrie believed in him.

Chapter
Thirty-Four

Carrie added the figures on the paper. The wheat and corn would bring a good price, come harvest. Mr. Dawson's demand for eggs was almost more than the hens could keep up with. And she had two new laundry customers and enough vegetables for winter store.

She re-added the columns and sat back in her chair. Next winter wasn't looking so bleak after all. The bank would get their money, and she would have a little to put away. Very little. But it was a start.

"Ma! Ma!" Nathan called from the kitchen door.

"What?" Carrie answered, without looking up from the table.

"Someone's comin'. I think it's Travis!"

"Nathan Lindquist, what have I told you about making up stories?"

"But... Ma, there really is somebody coming. Why don't you ever believe me?"

Carrie stood and met Nathan at the door. "Well, I'm sure it's not Travis. You know he's gone. We just have to accept that."

"Come on." He ran back to rejoin his sisters at the corner of the corral.

She strolled after him. The children shouldn't get so excited. Poor things. They had to accept the fact that Travis was gone. She walked up behind Nathan and put her hand on his shoulder.

"Well, you're right. There is a rider coming. But don't get your hopes up that it's Travis." They had to stop wishing.

"Doesn't that look like his horse, Ma?" Nathan pointed down the road.

"Yes, it does. But a lot of people own horses like that." But that was a man riding that roan. He did look a lot like… "Oh, stop this. You all need to quit staring and go back to what you were doing."

The roan horse with the lone rider turned into the yard.

"Travis!" Abigail ran to meet him as he dismounted.

Emily followed her big sister, squealing with delight.

"Travis! Travis! See, I told you, Ma!" Nathan hollered over his shoulder, as he ran to join the reunion.

Travis scooped Emily up in his arms, giving her a bear hug,

while Abigail hugged his leg. He patted her blond curls and then ruffled Nathan's hair.

"You came back!" Nathan observed the obvious. "Are you going to stay?"

"Well, that depends."

"On what?"

Travis set Emily down and turned his attention to her mother. "Hello, Carrie."

"Hello." They stood just feet apart. "I didn't expect to see you again. Did you forget something?"

"No. I, uh…" He fingered the reins. "Last night, I realized that for a long time I've been searching for something."

"What's that?"

"A place to start over. Even maybe a chance to practice medicine again." He shifted from one foot to the other.

"Oh, Travis, that's wonderful. I'm so happy for you."

"I already stopped in town and checked into opening an office. There's an empty building next to the freight office." His mischievous smile reached his eyes.

The smile that made her knees go weak. "Oh, that'll make Frank Robinson happy. Serves him right, I'd say." She giggled. Travis was staying in Cedar Creek? Well, at least he would be close.

"Yeah. But there's something else that I've been searching for even longer."

"Oh? And what is that? Have you found it?"

"I hope so." The muscle on his jaw twitched. "I've been looking for a home. A family. A place to settle down."

"Are you going to be our Papa?"

"Abigail!" Carrie shushed her daughter.

Travis looked like a nervous schoolboy, bringing his teacher flowers. "Well, if your ma will have me."

"What are you saying?" Carrie's heart spun like the new weathervane in the wind.

"Well, this isn't exactly how I planned it… but Carrie, will you marry me?" His face was red to the tops of his ears as he dropped his hands to his sides.

She felt like she had swallowed her tongue. "I… I don't know what to say. I didn't expect…"

"Say yes, Ma!" Nathan shouted.

Carrie looked from her son to Travis. She loved them both so very much. "Yes. Yes!"

"Yes, what?" he prodded her.

"Yes, Travis, I'll marry you!" She ran into his open arms.

He drew her to him and kissed her neck and then her cheek. She looked up at him. "What made you change your mind about leaving?"

"I realized that everything I've been looking for, all this time, is right here on this farm." He smiled that smile, and his lips met hers.

"Yeah! Mama and Travis are getting married!" Abigail danced and sang.

Emily tugged on her mother's skirt. "Is Tavis gonna stay?"

"You bet I am." Travis scooped her up in one arm and swept his other around Carrie's shoulder.

"You mean we're gonna be a family?" Nathan asked, a little disbelieving.

"Yes," Carrie smiled up at Travis, wiping tears from her cheeks. "Yes, we are."

Emily jumped down to join the revelry. Chester barked and chased the children as they danced around the couple.

"I'm so glad you came back," Carrie confessed. "I missed you so much. I was so afraid I'd never see you again. I love you so much." His arm felt so good around her. Big. Strong. Safe.

He turned her to face him. "Carrie Lindquist, I couldn't wait to get back here to see you. To thank you for believing in me. You made me believe in myself again."

"You made me believe, too. In you, and in God. Because of you, I believe that He really does love me."

"Carrie, that's wonderful!" He kissed her again, and she melted like candle wax.

Laying her head on his chest, she whispered, "I just can't believe you're here. I never dreamt that we could actually be together."

He hooked his finger under her chin, lifting her face to his. "I did," he grinned, with a twinkle in his eyes. Then, he squeezed her tighter and groaned. "You feel so wonderful in my arms. Just like I knew you would," he whispered in her ear. "I love you with all my heart."

She surrendered to his kiss and in that moment, heart to heart, they pledged their love forever.

About the Author

Glena (G.G.) Walker is a Colorado native. Her passion for story writing and western history was fueled on her grandparents' ranch, by family stories, and by exploring the mountains and western slope of Colorado.

She and her husband of thirty-eight years live in Pueblo and have two grown children and three grandchildren. Glena teaches in the preschool program at her church, loves to sing, especially with the worship team, is active in Bible study, and is a member of The Gideons International Auxiliary.

CPSIA information can be obtained
at www.ICGtesting.com
Printed in the USA
BVHW041758210920
589297BV00012B/133

9 781647 732493